# INTRODUCTION

If you asked most of us about the Book of Psalms, you would likely be greeted with a blank stare—"I really don't know anything about it." Actually we do.

The psalms have a remarkable way of turning up in the most unexpected places. Reporting on a rough stretch in President Clinton's first term, a writer at the *New York Times* wrote:

> Seeking solace from his recent political troubles, President Clinton said today that he has just read the entire Book of Psalms. . . . Friends, he said, have faxed him passages . . . on a daily basis . . . "During this difficult period, a lot of people were giving me different psalms to read," Mr. Clinton said. "It was amazing, and so I did." Mr. Clinton did not cite any particular psalms that had touched him. . . . Later, Mr. Stephanopoulos said the President cited five psalms as being important to him now: Psalms 25, 27, 90, 103 and 139.

In a biographical sketch in the *New Yorker* about Glenn Loury, one of America's foremost social scientists, Loury spoke about the moment when he turned his life from chaotic self-destruction to rediscovered purpose. He found himself committed to a mental institution.

> At McLean, Loury was visited by a pastor who prayed and read the Twenty-third Psalm with him. "Yea, though I walk through the valley of the shadow of death, I will fear no evil: for thou art with me": the words were familiar from childhood, but now he heard them differently. "For the first time in my life, I felt that I wasn't alone and that God could help," he says. That spring, he attended Easter services. As the organ swelled and the pastor preached, he thought of his sins and wept.

When Yitzchak Rabin, the Prime Minister of Israel, was assassinated in 1995, the Chief Rabbinate issued an appeal to all synagogue worshippers and school teachers, in all streams of Judaism, asking them to conduct a day of soul searching and to read chapters 121 and 130 of the Book of Psalms.

When terrorist bombs ripped through public buses in Jerusalem in 1996, reports from the scene noted that after dark, groups of mourners, most of them Orthodox Jews, gathered at the site to light memorial candles and to read psalms. Efrat Goldstein, a twenty-year-old Orthodox woman, stopped there to read Psalms on her way back home from work. "I felt that I had to," she said.

On the Op-Ed page of the *New York Times,* an American novelist living in Jerusalem wrote about the experiences of her twelve-year-old daughter in response to those tragic events.

> Hannah's costume parade was canceled. Instead, she and her classmates recited special Psalms for tragedy. Which ones? Twenty and 130. "I know them by heart," she said. "We say them so often these days. . . ."

The Book of Psalms is part of the cultural life of our society as well. Phrases from Psalms float around our heads: "By the rivers of Babylon"; "Yea, though I walk through the valley of the shadow of death"; "the stone which the builders rejected"; "the dead cannot praise God." We all recognize snatches of psalms. At symphony concerts we hear the words of the psalms set to music by some of the world's greatest composers, including Beethoven, Mozart, Ravel, Stravinsky, and Bernstein to name only a few. The psalms have entered into our common cultural vocabulary. They have done so because they are beautiful and powerful as literature, and because what they have to say is charged with the capacity to stir us and move our imaginations—and our souls.

Thanks to the presence of the psalms in so many aspects of our lives—our society, our politics, our culture—you are probably more familiar with them than you realize. We also encounter psalms every time we attend worship services at a synagogue or church. Psalms form the backbone of the Jewish prayer book. Entire psalms are included in the liturgy, and the language and concerns of psalms established the pattern that shaped many of the prayers in our worship service. Indeed, many scholars have conjectured that worship services evolved from the regular recitation of psalms during the period of the Babylonian Exile, when the Jewish people were not able to perform the sacrificial rites at the Temple in Jerusalem.

## What Makes the Psalms So Beloved?

So we do know about the psalms after all. But most of us don't know what is contained in them—and the source of their hold on us. What is the power of these ancient poems? What is the pull they exercise on people, the pull that causes people to read them over and over again, the pull that long ago led people to evolve the worship service itself so that they could visit—and reinterpret—psalms regularly? The power of the psalms is the major focus of this book.

One clue to the power of the Book of Psalms can be found in the life of a well-known contemporary hero of the Jewish people, former Soviet refusenik Anatoly Sharansky, who became Natan Sharansky when he emigrated to Israel in 1986. Sharansky had been held prisoner by Soviet authorities, detained in solitary confinement for years with nothing to read but his Book of Psalms. When his release was finally negotiated and he was exchanged for a Soviet spy, Sharansky insisted on taking his Book of Psalms with him, refusing repeated efforts by his former jailers to take it away from him. He carried Psalms with him as he crossed the bridge to freedom, held it aloft when he finally arrived in Jerusalem, and made his way with it directly to the Western Wall.

Writing about his imprisonment, Sharansky's wife Avital said,

"Anatoly has been educated to his Jewishness in a lonely cell in Chistopol Prison, where locked alone with the Psalms of David, he found expression for his innermost feelings in the outpourings of the king of Israel thousands of years ago."

In his love of the psalms, and in finding his deepest feelings given voice in the psalms, Sharansky was the embodiment of every Jew for the last three thousand years, and every Christian, too. Somehow the psalms put us in touch with what matters most to us, and express those feelings more clearly and movingly than we can express them ourselves.

More than any other part of scripture, we can say that the psalms are not beloved because they are holy, but that they are holy because they are beloved. We do not turn to psalms out of a sense of obligation. We read psalms because they help us confront the pains and challenges that are part of every human life. Psalms help us put into words what we experience and feel; more than that, many will tell you, psalms help us overcome our problems and bear the burdens that life places on all of us.

What has made the psalms so beloved and powerful is not their divinity, but their humanity. Psalms grew out of the soil of human experience. They talk to us in the voice of a fellow journeyer along life's path, and they have within them the resources to help us when the journey gets difficult.

## Becoming Friends with the Book of Psalms

As we explore what the psalms have to offer, our main goal is not to understand the world in which they were composed. Instead, we will read psalms to find the light they can shed on our lives. In other words, we will study psalms not to become experts in psalms, but to let psalms help us understand more about ourselves. In fact we will strive to become friends with psalms so that we can turn to them as true friends for help in our times of need.

Each of us brings our own particular experience to everything each of us does. Our histories and struggles shape the way we see our world and the way we understand everything we study. No book of the Bible lends itself as much as Psalms does to being read through the lenses of our own circumstances and search.

The Book of Psalms talks to our spiritual quest: our desire to find God and our frustration that God often seems remote, hidden, unapproachable, and unknowable. Psalms talks to human pain—illness and fear, and to the sense that we sometimes have of being abandoned. Psalms knows the sting of failure and the distress of being betrayed by people we trusted. Psalms can be the voice through which we cry out for help, and Psalms can be the guide through which the lost begin to be found.

In Psalms we watch the drama of salvation enacted—not salvation on the grand cosmological scale, but the simple story of people saved from the burdens that oppressed them.

Psalms talks of thanksgiving—breaking out in shouts of joy and gratitude when darkness that threatened to envelop us is pierced by rays of hope. Psalms shows us the path to triumph and provides the songs to sing when we have prevailed.

Psalms does all of this as any friend should—without lecturing, demanding, or coercing. Psalms teaches us by example, by showing us, "I've been there, that has happened to me, and this is how I made it through."

The personal message of the Book of Psalms is the reason people have turned to it for thousands of years. It is the power latent in Psalms that has made it the first refuge of people in distress. That power has not diminished over time. It remains ever-present and available to us, if we know how to find it. Turning to the Book of Psalms, learning where to look and how to understand it, is a study we undertake not from some lofty, theoretical vantage, but from the very human need to make our lives better, more at ease, and whole. We are drawn to Psalms, as generations before us were, not by abstract curiosity, but by the compulsion—not figurative, but literal—to save our lives.

Psalms still holds the power to help us through the darkest times, give us our bearings, and enrich our lives. Sadly for too many of us today, when we say, "We do not know anything about Psalms," it is that power of which we are ignorant. This book is an attempt to help today's readers rediscover the whole-making power of the psalms.

# A Word about the Translation

The translation that I have employed in this book is almost entirely from the Jewish Publication Society translation of *The Holy Scriptures* (1917). In a very few instances I have modified the translation for clarity.

The JPS has published a more recent translation (*Tanakh,* 1985); but I prefer the older one for its more poetic quality, the majesty of its language, the graphic quality of the images, and the cadence of its verses.

The older translation makes use of what we today recognize as "masculine language" in speaking about God. This is in marked contrast to the language I have employed throughout the book; I hope you, the reader, will find as I do that the poetic quality of the older JPS translation is worth the price of this dissonance.

# 1

# WHAT ARE THE PSALMS?

**B**efore we explore the psalms and the pull they have had on people throughout the generations, let us learn something about this remarkable book, where it came from, and what it has meant in peoples' lives.

The Book of Psalms (*Tehillim* in Hebrew, *Tillim* in Yiddish) is found in *K'tuvim,* the third section of the *Tanach* (Jewish Bible).\* *K'tuvim* (Writings) is a miscellany of various and varied literature, including the Song of Songs, the Book of Esther, Lamentations, and the "wisdom literature" of *Koheleth* (Ecclesiastes), Proverbs, and Job. What these works have in common is that they are not sacred history such as we find in the Torah and parts of *Nevi'im* (Prophets), nor are they accounts of divine revelation such as we find in *Nevi'im.* Rather, books of *K'tuvim* are religious teachings, or intended for use in worship settings. Psalms fits both of these criteria.

---

\**TaNaCH* is the acronym formed from the first letters of the names of the three sections of the Hebrew Bible: Torah (the Five Books), *Nevi'im* (Prophets), and *K'tuvim* (Writings).

The Book of Psalms is made up of 150 individual poetic compositions. Each psalm is separate and discrete, and is often referred to as a chapter in the book. The various psalms, or chapters, are of differing lengths. They differ as well in tone, style, mood, and subject matter. By and large, there is no connection between a psalm and the ones before and after it, although there are a few instances of thematic linkage among adjacent psalms.

The Book of Psalms is divided into *five* books, although there is no real continuity or connection between these five sub-sections. It has been suggested that the division into five books was imposed upon the text when it was edited and set down in its final form to make it parallel in structure to the Five Books of Moses. Certainly reading any of these books on its own adds nothing to our understanding of the individual psalms or of the Book of Psalms as a whole.

The Book of Psalms is best appreciated as a collection of religious poems, or even prayers of varying poetic quality, although for the most part the quality is compellingly, even dauntingly, high. Though certain themes, images, and phrases are repeated in more than one psalm, we can get the most from the book if we treat the various psalms individually, rather than try to force the entire work into an ideological unity. True, we will find a certain resonance in concerns and images repeated in various places, but we would diminish the book if we presented it as one consistent voice. The Book of Psalms and the various books within it do not say just *one* thing. The psalms say *many* things, which is what makes the book so complex, as well as so rewarding. Religiously, we gain by engaging with 150 separate psalms instead of a single Book of Psalms.

We do not have to think of the "Book" in the Book of Psalms as having a capital "B" (which the Book of Genesis and the Book of Exodus certainly do). It is more like the use of the word "book" in the phrase "a book of pictures" or "a book of poetry." The Book of Psalms is the library in which these distinct works are housed.

## *King David and the Psalms*

Traditionally, Psalms is said to have been written by King David. In the Talmud we read:

> David composed a hundred and three chapters [of Psalms], and he did not say "Hallelujah" until he saw the downfall of the wicked, as it says, "Let sinners cease out of the earth, and let the wicked be no more. Bless the Lord, O my soul. Hallelujah." Now are these a hundred and three? Are they not a hundred and four? You must assume therefore that "Happy is the man" and "Why are the nations in an uproar" form one chapter. For R. Samuel b. Nahmani said in the name of R. Johanan: [10a]: Every chapter that was particularly dear to David he commenced with "Happy" and terminated with "Happy". He began with "Happy", as it is written "Happy is the man", and he terminated with "Happy", as it is written "happy are all they that take refuge in Him." (Berachot 9b–10a)

Indeed, the Book of Psalms is frequently referred to as the Psalms of David.

*Midrash Tehillim,* a medieval commentary on the Book of Psalms says:

> Moses gave Israel the Five Books of the Torah and correspondingly, David gave them the Five Books of Psalms.

In our own time, Israeli Nobel Prize–winning author S. Y. Agnon, in extolling the Book of Psalms, invokes King David to attest to its importance. Agnon writes:

> They contain everything. Nothing is more important than the Book of Psalms. King David asked that those who read

Psalms should receive the same reward as they would receive if they were engaged in the depths of the Torah.

There is a lovely *midrash*—a rabbinic story—about King David. It is said that when David went to sleep at night, he hung his harp over his bed. As he slept, the four winds came and plucked the strings of his harp. David would awake and sing along. According to the story, these songs became the psalms.

Why did King David's association with Psalms arise? The most obvious reason is that out of the 150 psalms, seventy-three begin with the superscription (introductory phrase) *L'David*. The most obvious translation of the phrase *L'David* is "of David," although it also has various other meanings, which we will discuss shortly. At this point, however, suffice it to note that the phrase was taken to mean that these seventy-three psalms were *of David*, and thus *by David*. By extension, the work as a whole was attributed to him.

The Book of Psalms can also be attributed to David because the very literary form of the work fits nicely with what we know about him. The biography of David contained in the two Books of Samuel tells us a number of things that connect him to this work. In his youth David was a skillful lyre player and an inventor of musical instruments. He is said to have been a composer of songs and won his first public recognition as a singer. He was acclaimed as the "sweet singer of Israel." Later, he is said to have been responsible for organizing the guilds of Temple singers and musicians.

Another reason for ascribing the Book of Psalms to King David is that many of the psalms portray circumstances and emotional states that harmonize with what we read about David's life in the books of First and Second Samuel and First

Kings. Some commentators have gone so far as to suggest that Psalms 1–72 should be read collectively as a biography of David. This particular approach often requires a stretch of such dimensions as to leave the reader intellectually contorted. It also leaves us knowing virtually nothing about the details and specifics of the life of King David, which has been richly chronicled elsewhere in *Tanach.*

But it is possible to associate some of the psalms with specific aspects of the life of David. Psalm 2 is easily linked to the establishment of the Davidic dynasty. The shepherd motif of Psalm 23 and other psalms can certainly be connected with David's occupation in his youngest days. Psalm 110 can be read as depicting David's coronation as king. Most notably, Psalm 18 is duplicated in its entirety in 2 Samuel, Chapter 22. Jewish tradition found this association with the life of King David so compelling that much of the commentary on the Book of Psalms—such as the *Midrash Tehillim,* the literary explication on Psalms—is devoted to associating particular psalms to events in David's life.

Modern scholarship suggests that King David may not have written all of the psalms, or any of them. What can be stated with certainty is that many of the psalms originated in a time much later than David's lifetime (which was around 1000 B.C.E.). Many appear to come from the time when the first Temple was standing, which was well after David's death. Some reflect specific historic events from later periods. Most famously, Psalm 137 talks about the Babylonian Exile—hundreds of years after David's death (586 B.C.E.). Others portray the return of the exiles to Jerusalem, the rebuilding of the Temple, and perhaps even its dedication (540 B.C.E.). Unless one wants to believe that David wrote psalms foretelling these events, we must at least recognize that these psalms could not have come from his hand.

The fact is that normative Jewish teaching tends not to take seriously the tradition that David wrote the Book of Psalms. An interesting exchange is found in the Talmud:

> It is taught, Rabbi Meir used to say, "all the praises stated in the book of Psalms, David uttered all of them" . . . Who recited the *Hallel* [Psalms 113–118]? Rabbi Yose said, "My son Eliezer argues that it was recited by Moses and all the Israelites when they crossed the [Red] sea, but his colleagues disagree with him, maintaining that David . . . [wrote] it. Clearly his view is preferable to theirs . . ." (Pesachim 117a)

Interestingly, Rabbi Yose's opinion is not unique in the Talmud. By and large the Talmud recognizes the Book of Psalms as a collection of works by different authors.

> Who wrote the scriptures? . . . David wrote the Book of Psalms, including in it the work of the elders, namely, Adam, Melchizedek, Abraham, Moses, Heman, Yoduthan, Asaph, and the three sons of Korah. (Baba Bathra 14b–15a)

Medieval commentators are, likewise, comfortable acknowledging the later date of many of the psalms.

When we find the phrase *L'David,* we can understand it in various ways. It does not have to mean *of David* or *by David.* It can also mean *concerning David*—a later composition reflecting on some aspect of the life of David. The phrase can mean *in the style of David*—a composition similar to what David wrote in his time. We can even conjecture that *L'David* can be translated as *to David*—composed by members of a guild of musicians that traced itself back to David.

Indeed the majority of the psalms do not even bear the superscription *L'David.* In fact, many of them bear superscriptions attributing them to other authors: the "sons of Korach," Asaph,

Ethan the Ezrahite, and even Solomon and Moses. As we noted, many of the psalms are clearly from later periods of time. Jewish tradition does not require us to accept all of the psalms as having been written by King David, nor does it seriously argue that the Book of Psalms was composed by him.

## How Did the Psalms Find Their Way into Our Religious Life?

What, then, are the psalms? As with so much in Jewish religious practice, the psalms involve a borrowing from our neighbors. Like the story of the Flood, the Temple, the institution of the priest-hood, and so much else, the Book of Psalms involved a reframing of other peoples' religious practices to fit our own ideology. Psalms incorporates pieces of Canaanite poetry, and there are literary connections to poems and hymns of various Mesopotamian cultures. In his magisterial translation of Psalms in the Anchor Bible series, Mitchell Dahoud finds significance in Psalms' resemblance to the collections of ancient Ugaritic poetry. Jews did not invent the literary style of Psalms. We borrowed it, and made it our own.

Similarly, the psalms do not speak in a single voice, or of a single subject matter. The psalms sing of many things. Some serve as hymns, giving poetic expression to religious commitments: praise, petition, and supplication on behalf of the nation or of the individual. Others focus on the issues of sin, atonement, and for-giveness. Some psalms are poetic expressions of what we could call the national mythology. They devote themselves to a retelling of the people's history. There are psalms that give voice to con-cerns of a particular moment—the present moment—in the life of the nation. Numbers of psalms could be said to serve an almost didactic purpose: They teach ideals and values in much the same way as the "wisdom literature" found elsewhere in *K'tuvim*. Still other psalms speak in the same terms as the Prophets, denouncing evil behavior and oppression.

The psalms are patterned on non-Israelite literary models, and give voice to a wide range of concerns: How did they find their way into our religious life? It is quite possible that they were connected to Temple worship and the sacrificial cult. Many scholars have argued vehemently and cogently that no such connection existed. But based on what we know of the practice of sacrifice in other ancient religious traditions and in various cultures in which it continues to be practiced, it seems extremely unlikely that the sacrifices at the Temple in Jerusalem were conducted in deathly silence. The great scholar of Jewish liturgy and music, A. Z. Idelsohn, maintains that while the sacrifices burned on the altar, the Levites sang psalms accompanied by instruments.

In the discussion in *Pesachim* 117a cited earlier, Rabbi Yose makes very much this same argument for his assertion—anachronistic though it was—that Moses and the Israelites composed the *Hallel* (Psalms 113–118).

> My son, Eliezer, argues that it [the *Hallel*] was recited by Moses and all the Israelites when they crossed the [Red] Sea, but his colleagues disagree with him, maintaining that David . . . [wrote] it. Clearly his view is preferable to theirs: is it possible that Israel slaughtered their Passover offerings . . . without uttering song?

What is of interest here is not the idea Rabbi Yose is trying to prove, but the argument he makes on behalf of his claim. Rabbi Yose, closer to the time and realities of the sacrificial cult than we, took it as a matter of course that sacrifice would be accompanied by psalms. This seems likely to have been the case.

While we cannot know the origins of the psalms with certainty, it is clear that they eventually became a religious phenomenon unto themselves. We know that the tradition that there were 150 psalms was established very early, even if there was no consistent tradition about the identity or arrangement of those psalms. The existence of the five books of psalms within the greater book, and the repetition of a few psalms in different parts of those books, allows us to speculate that prior to the final codification of Psalms, a number of collections existed that ultimately became joined into the Book of Psalms we read today. Certainly people developed a deep attachment to the psalms, and it is likely that this attachment led to the codification of a definitive collection.

Why the psalms were composed or how the Book of Psalms was compiled is not our greatest concern. As we gain a better understanding of the sources that shaped this text, what is most striking is the development of the Book of Psalms as an important element in the religious life of the Jewish people. Indeed, it became a beloved part of the lives of individual Jews. In time people began not merely reading the psalms, but putting the psalms to use. That is a tradition well worth recovering in our own day.

# 2

# THE POWER OF PSALMS

. . . With a clatter the trunk rolled right into the synagogue!

A near panic broke out among the worshippers. Their shrieks and screams were heard by the women and children, who came to see what was happening in the house of worship.

Strange voices were heard inside the trunk. Helm became frightened . . . surely the trunk was full of demons! The congregation stood petrified, and the Rabbi was about to begin reciting Psalms . . .[1]

What a strange moment, indeed, to begin the study of sacred text. Yet this is what is described in a well-known folktale. And in a recent news report we find the following account:

Some 33,000 Doenmeh, or secret Sabbateans, live in Turkey. Their calendar for secret religious observance

includes conventional Jewish holidays such as Rosh
Hashanah and Yom Kippur—and less orthodox ones such
as the Festival of Light, when groups of married couples
meet in a private home, slaughter a lamb, chant Psalms,
and then swap partners . . .[2]

Once again, a most unlikely moment for the study of scripture.

The fact is, of course, that Jews do not "study" psalms the
same way we study other texts. Our relationship with this book is
different from that with any other book in the Bible. Historically,
it has been the custom for Jews to have copies of the Book of
Psalms—often very small volumes—with them at all times to turn
to in moments of trouble. These little volumes of *Tillim*, along
with copies of the *Tanach* and the Prayer Book, were often a Jew's
most precious possessions.

The Jewish people has always felt a special affinity for the
Book of Psalms. The Talmud says that it was the will of the people
at large that forced the Rabbis to formalize the practice of assign-
ing a particular psalm to each day of the week. Thus it is now for-
mal dictate, and not just popular custom, that gives every day its
own psalm. Mishna Tamid 7:4 gives us the order that is followed
to this day:

| | |
|---|---|
| Sunday | Psalm 24 |
| Monday | Psalm 48 |
| Tuesday | Psalm 82 |
| Wednesday | Psalm 94 |
| Thursday | Psalm 81 |
| Friday | Psalm 93 |
| Shabbat | Psalm 92 |

Behind this practice lies the real question of why the people have, and have always had, such profound devotion to the Book of Psalms. Here is where we begin to confront the real power of the psalms. The power of the psalms is that they speak directly and personally to the human condition. In *Midrash Tehillim* (to Psalm 18:1) Rabbi Yudan says in the name of Rabbi Judah, "Whatever David says in his book pertains to himself, to all Israel and to all times." The same appreciation of the power of the psalms is articulated in the Christian tradition by one of the Church Fathers, Athanasius, Bishop of Alexandria (C.E. 293?–373):

> The Psalms embrace the entire human life, express every emotion of the soul, every impulse of the heart—[The Psalms speak for you] when the soul yearns for penance and confession, when thy spirit is depressed or joyous . . . when thy soul is yearning to express its thanks to God, or its pains . . .

Both Rabbi Judah and Bishop Athanasius identify that essential quality of the psalms that has made them so beloved, and so powerful. The psalms are remarkably human. They validate the whole range of human emotions. Psalms start with the recognition of just how tenuous life is: we suffer; we experience fear and exaltation; we meet with success and failure; we know contentment and anxiety; we experience betrayal, have enemies, even know rage and the desire for revenge; and we find vindication, comfort, new confidence. The psalms give voice to all of these emotions and help us put them in context. They help us marshal our resources so that we can move from hurt to healing, from the valley of the shadow back to the high places of life. The psalms hold out hope for us, even in our darkest hours. Above all, the psalms encourage us to give voice to our emotions and pour our hearts out to God.

## Seeing God in the Psalms

Human emotions are real and vibrant in the psalms, and so is the living presence of God. The psalms present us with a vivid sense of God's nearness. The nature of the experience of God in Psalms is congruent with the experience that most of us have in our own lives. In Torah and Prophets the story is almost always about God reaching out to people, something most of us do not experience directly most of the time. The psalms are about people reaching out to God, which is what we do experience, or what we can aspire to do. The psalms are a model for us of what our relationship with God can be. They show the close intimacy we can develop.

From another perspective, Psalms presents a compelling image of God. The God of the psalms is close at hand, listens, and is *chasid*—steadfast, reliable. The God of the psalms is a God who cares. We are assured that God cares about God's people (111:9) and that God cares about individuals. Religiously, this is the most compelling aspect of the psalms. God not only cares about the people as a whole, the great leaders, and the religious teachers, but also about individuals, average ordinary people, and perhaps especially, those who are cast down and hurting.

In Psalms, God is close by (34:19). God guards our going out and coming in—always (121:8). God listens (116:1). The ear of God is inclined to hear us. God is near to all who call on God (145:18). God champions the needy and downtrodden. God raises the poor from the dust (113:7).

Psalms assures us that God saves us, rescues us. Seventy-six times in the 150 psalms we are assured of God's ability and desire to save us. Because of this, the religious lesson of psalms is the lesson of hope—hope and *religious* patience: "I wait for the Lord, my soul doth wait, and in God's word do I hope." (130:5)

The relationship with God that psalms models for us is intimate and intense. We can make demands on God, and be clear

and explicit in what we want. Indeed, the closeness of the relationship even allows us to challenge God. As we pour out our
hearts and our needs to God, we can even chastise God for the
pains and difficulties that have befallen us.

Psalms teaches us that the greatest happiness is being in
God's presence. Ultimately, the recitation of psalms becomes per-
formative—that is, the very act of reciting them fulfills the goal to
which they aspire. Reciting *tillim* puts us in contact with God,
brings us into God's presence. The very recitation of psalms in
itself brings us happiness.

## Using Psalms for Sacred Moments

For these reasons, the psalms have become so precious to the
Jewish people, and the recitation of psalms a customary part of
sacred moments. Psalms are recited with a woman when she is in
childbirth, and with a baby boy the night before his circumci-
sion. When a child is given her or his name, it is the practice to
take appropriate verses from Psalm 119—in which the verses are
arranged in alphabetical order—and create an acrostic of the
child's name. Among the Jews of Yemen, psalms are recited with
a boy the night before he becomes bar mitzvah. Universally in
the Jewish world, psalms are recited at the bedside of a person
who is close to death. When a person dies, someone is assigned
to remain with the body, reciting psalms, until it is buried.
Psalms are the central part of the funeral service, and are recited as we accompany the body to the cemetery. You could say that
whenever Jews hold a vigil of any kind, psalms are at the core of
the experience.

In many parts of the world, it is customary to recite the entire
Book of Psalms on the night of Yom Kippur. In describing this custom, S. Y. Agnon adds words of praise for psalms that can apply to

all occasions on which psalms are recited. His tribute captures the special esteem in which psalms are held, and the devotion Jews feel to them:

> It is the custom in many parts of the Exile to recite all the Book of Psalms on the night of Yom Kippur. This is a good custom for those who are conscientious, for there is nothing more important than the Book of Psalms, which contains everything . . . and all the Psalms come from the hand of God.[3]

## What About "Magical" Uses of Psalms?

There is one other dimension of the Jews' devotion to the psalms that demands our attention. Much has been written about the relationship of religion and magic. It has often been noted that there is a continuum that runs between the realm of the strictly religious, and the realm of the "magical." Any specific act, under differing circumstances, can be placed at different points along that continuum. The same act can be performed for religious or for magical purposes—kissing the *mezuzah* in the Jewish tradition or doing honor to a statue of Saint Joseph in the Roman Catholic tradition. It should not surprise us that the psalms have become so central to the spiritual lives of Jews, that they are often put to use to serve purposes that might be described as magical.

Thus the reading of psalms in the two episodes described at the beginning of this chapter. The rabbi in the story about the village of Helm was not engaged in study—or even prayer—when he began to recite psalms as he approached the presumably demon-inhabited trunk. Rather, he hoped to make use of the power of psalms to protect himself as he neared this fearsome object, and to protect his community from the effects of its presence.

And the Doenmeh of Turkey? What we know of their beliefs and practices tells us that their "swapping" of partners is not an act of licentiousness or hedonistic excess (if romance was the goal, they would be reading the Song of Songs). It is an act with resolute purpose. Instead of having pleasure as its goal, this aberrant practice is undertaken in the hope that "out of one of these adulterous unions, the reincarnation of Shabtai Tzvi [the false messiah whose career inspired the founders of this sect] will be born."[4] Doubtless such a self-consciously reprehensible act would be entered into with fear and trembling. It seems unlikely that the participants would interrupt the proceedings to engage in some Torah study. More likely, psalms would be recited to protect the participants from the consequences of the sinful dimensions of their undertaking; or perhaps in the hope that they would aid in fixing their minds on the more "sacred" intent of the act. Psalms are once again not studied, but invoked for their magical powers. This use of psalms is familiar beyond these specific instances. Indeed it is quite widespread.

The great Chasidic teacher, Rabbi Nachman of Breslov, made special use of the psalms in a way that tends toward the magical side of the spectrum. One of Nachman's teachings was the *Tikkun C'lali*—the complete or all-purpose remedy. Nachman prescribed his remedy for people afflicted by impure thoughts. He taught that such people had only to recite ten designated psalms on the same day as the impure occurrence, and the sin would be completely rectified. The ten psalms that constituted Rabbi Nachman's *Tikkun C'lali* are Psalms 16, 32, 41, 42, 59, 77, 90, 105, 137, and 150. It is possible that such recitation of ten psalms had less to do with the content of those psalms than with some protective quality associated with the very act of reciting them.

Even more magical in purpose was the Kabbalistic custom of including selected psalms in amulets and talismans, reflecting the belief that the very words of psalms had the power to keep at bay the forces that would harm us. The use of such amulets and talismans is said to have been extremely widespread and accorded great popularity.[5] In addition to their protective quality, there was popular belief that the recitation of psalms could bring desired results. Thus we learn that when you are praying for rain you should recite Psalms 17, 25, 32, 86, 103, 105, 108, 120, 121, 123, 124, 130 and 136 followed by the prayer *yehi ratzon* (may it be Your will).

At the apex of the magical approach to psalms is a medieval book called *Shimush Tehillim* (The [Magical] Use of Psalms). The premise of this book is the belief that the entire Torah is composed of the names of God, and that in consequence, it has the property of saving and protecting people. *Shimush Tehillim* identifies a specific magical purpose to which each psalm can be put. It maintains that the recitation of particular psalms can help people protect themselves from certain identified dangers, or help them attain certain desired goals. As examples from *Shimush Tehillim*, we are instructed to use:

- Psalm 14 or 38 to protect yourself against defamation or when your veracity is doubted
- Psalm 18 to protect yourself against sickness—also robbers
- Psalm 22 to sharpen your intelligence
- Psalm 28 to appease an enemy
- Psalms 25 and 26 when in distress
- Psalm 111 to gain a new friend
- Psalm 114 to be fortunate in business
- Psalm 138 for love

Here, as with Rabbi Nachman of Breslov's *Tikkun C'lali*, there is no apparent logical connection between the purpose to which a particular psalm is designated and its manifest context. What is significant in both cases is that the psalms were employed for the well-being of the person reading them.

The fact that the psalms have been put to magical use at various times and in various contexts should not diminish our sense of their majesty—or their importance. These magical uses of psalms are an extreme manifestation of the underlying reality of the relationship Jews have to them. We do not simply study psalms; we make use of them.

Even without the more magical approach, Jews have always looked to psalms for the help they offer. More than any other part of the Bible, psalms touch the reality of our day-to-day existence, and have the power to enrich the spiritual quality of our lives. They can be woven into the tapestry of every moment, and give perspective and meaning to every experience. They help us get in touch with ourselves, our emotional reactions to the events of our lives, and our needs. They aid us in finding solace, strength, and hope. They assist us at every moment as we reach out to God, the eternal Thou and Answerer of our needs.

# 3

*This Is the Lord's Doing; It Is Marvelous in Our Eyes*

# REVERSAL OF FORTUNE

Hers was a romantic story—and a tragic one. She met a man she loved deeply, but had to wait because her sister married him. Finally, after a long wait, she, too, married him. She knew the most extreme kind of sororial conflict with her sister. She knew longing, envy, passion, rage, despair, and delight. She died when she was still very young, but the image of her remained with her husband until the moment of his death decades later.

The story of Rachel, known as Rachel *imanu* (Rachel our mother), is well known; we read her story in Genesis chapters 29–35. It is so compelling in its emotional intensity that it touches all of us who read it, and stays with us as part of our own personal myth system.

We recall that Jacob fled from his home fearing the wrath of his aggrieved brother Esau. Soon after he entered his family's ancestral homeland he met Rachel, his cousin. They were in love from the moment they laid eyes on each other. When she introduced him to her father Laban, Laban proposed that Jacob work for him for seven years to earn Rachel's hand. Jacob agreed eagerly and, as the biblical text expresses so evocatively, "Jacob worked those seven years for Rachel, yet they seemed as only a few days in his eyes, such was his love for her." (Genesis 29:20)

We remember, too, how Laban tricked Jacob. When the wedding day finally arrived, Laban arranged to have Jacob wed Rachel's older sister Leah. Jacob worked yet another seven years and, in keeping with the polygamous social patterns of that day, was able to wed Rachel as well, and to acquire the sisters' handmaids as his concubines.

At this point, the story seems to have achieved the proverbial "happy ending." And yet, rather than live happily ever after, Rachel entered into a prolonged period of what must be recognized as wrenching frustration and longing. Much as she wanted to have a child with her beloved Jacob, she remained barren, and watched in building resentment as her sister and the two handmaids conceived child after child.

The Bible talks candidly about Rachel's pain. "As Rachel saw that she could not bear any children for Jacob, her anger was consumed with jealousy against her sister." (Genesis 30:1) The more she saw their joy and fulfillment, the more embittered she became. The text makes clear how her despair strained her relations with Jacob. How many couples struggling with infertility can hear their own desperation echoed in this episode: "(Rachel) said to Jacob, 'Give me children and if not I am as dead.' And Jacob's anger blazed against Rachel, and he said, 'Am I in the place of God, that I can withhold from you the fruit of the womb?'" (Genesis 30:1–2) In Rachel boiled an explosive mixture of love, yearning, disappointment, jealousy, and the most profound kind of hurt.

Rachel's desire for a child, and her frustration, echo the agony experienced by so many other women in the Torah, including the other matriarchs, Sarah and Rebecca, and, elsewhere in the Bible, the mother of Samson, and Hannah, the mother of Samuel.

The Bible writes with empathy and compassion about the depths of despair these women experienced, the doubt each of them felt, and the very human impulse each had to share a child with her husband. Each of them yearned for the love a mother feels for her child. Their sense of frustration and unfulfillment was also heightened by the realities of the society in which they lived, where a woman's very well-being was dependent on bearing children—and more specifically, a son. A woman who had no son when her husband died was left without a protector in a world that could be predatory and cruel. She was, at best, dependent on the kindness of her family and community; at worst, defenseless in the face of countless adversities and perils.

To be without a son in such a society was to face emotional deprivation and physical threat. All the more complicated when your sister-rival, her surrogate, and your own handmaid were successfully accomplishing the one thing you most longed for.

## What Does Reversal of Fortune Mean for Us?

It seems that none of us can get through life without episodes in which things do not work out as planned. Indeed, we will most likely have times when we feel we are in actual jeopardy. Every part of our life is subject to collapse—our relationships, careers, health. We can be emotionally starved or economically threatened. Our jobs may not work out, and our very bodies can fail us, even threaten us.

At these moments we are Rachel. Everyone else seems to be living rich, fulfilling lives, radiant with joy and success, while we are failing and falling into peril. In these times when we are

Rachel, our lives seem utterly without hope. We feel threatened beyond redemption. We cannot imagine who or what could pull us up out of the pit that our lives have become. We have, in our own eyes, literally bottomed out, and we see no way up. As another of the matriarchs, Rebecca, cried out in the midst of her own travail, "If this is how it will be for me, how can I go on living?" (Genesis 25:22)

The experience of being at the end of our rope is vividly evoked in so many of the psalms, as we have already seen. But despair and even rage do not exhaust the experience of Rachel. For despair is not the end of her story.

On the journey of Rachel's life there still awaits a high place of happiness. Later, in the same chapter that began with her despair, envy, and rage, we read:

> God remembered Rachel and God heard her, and opened up her womb. She conceived and gave birth to a son. She said God has withdrawn my humiliation. She named him Yosef [Joseph] meaning, through me has God added (Yosef) another son.          (Genesis 30:22–24)

When we are being Rachel, when we are in the pit, it seems impossible to imagine that our journey might hold more in store for us. As our lives seem to spiral downward, we cannot envision a time in which the course of our trajectory could turn around. It is to this very state of mind that the Book of Psalms speaks so powerfully.

Many of the psalms speak directly to a phenomenon we can call "reversal of fortune." The Book of Psalms has given solace to generations of Jews because it speaks of precisely this movement. When we feel ourselves in a downward slide, Psalms assures us that our course can be reversed. When we feel lost, it talks to us of becoming found. When we are alone, it reminds us that we can again become part of a community. Reversal of fortune is one of the hallmarks of Psalms, and one of the reasons Psalms is so beloved.

Indeed many of the individual psalms seem intentionally crafted to allow us to experience the movement of descent and ascent, of falling and rising again. In many of the psalms, the very structure of the psalm bespeaks a reversal of fortune, a change of circumstance. Many psalms not only attest to the notion that fortune can be reversed, but also afford us the opportunity to experience that shift and feel our way into how it could work in our own lives.

Viewed from one perspective so many of the psalms function as drama: We actually see events unfold before us. Within certain psalms we experience internal movement. These psalms do not merely give voice to despair, or cry out for help; they actually reveal movement toward overcoming the cause of that despair. And we, through reading these psalms, feel ourselves caught up in that movement. Because the psalms pull us into their movement by making us players in these dramas of reversal of fortune, we are assured that we can experience the same kind of movement in the dramas of our own lives. This is an important aspect to the power of the psalms.

## *Moving with Rachel from Despair to Joy*

Because we began with the story of Rachel, our first close reading is a section of a psalm that seems to have her, and all of our anguished matriarchs, in its heart. Psalm 113 moves from the depths of degradation to the heights of fulfillment, and ends on a note of exaltation, rejoicing in precisely that reversal of fortune.

[5]Who is like unto the Lord our God,
  That is enthroned on high,
[6]That looketh down low
  Upon heaven and upon earth?
[7]Who raiseth up the poor out of the dust,
  And lifteth up the needy out of the dunghill;
[8]That He may set him with princes,
  Even with the princes of His people.
[9]Who maketh the barren woman to dwell in her house
  As a joyful mother of children.
  Hallelujah.

In these wonderful verses, you can almost feel the promise of change of direction with the Psalm's balance of high (verse 5) and low (verse 6), heaven and earth, before it even begins to talk about our lives and the complexities we human beings face. Once it does, it speaks in graphic images—a man so poor, he is, or feels like he is, cast on the garbage heap. That man does not remain in the refuse bin. He gets lifted up and joins the elite of his own society.

Swiftly, within one concluding verse, this psalm catches all the despair and ultimate exaltation of the story of Rachel and so many others. In five simple words, the barren woman becomes "the joyous mother of children." How can we not conclude, as the psalmist does, "Hallelujah" (praise to God)?

Of course, the psalm is not merely about that poor man or the barren woman. It is about all of us who identify with them, or have felt ourselves in their place. And it is about the promise that the reversal of fortune that occurred to them can happen to us.

## *Understanding Reversal of Fortune in Our Lives: Looking to the Psalms*

The sense of confidence and hope is hardly confined to this psalm. Indeed, it is echoed in the very first verse of the psalm that follows it. Psalm 114 is a joyous meditation on the Exodus from Egypt. The first words—"When Israel came forth . . ."—celebrate a reversal of fortune of unprecedented magnitude.

1When Israel came forth out of Egypt,
  The house of Jacob from a people of strange language;
2Judah became His sanctuary,
  Israel His dominion.
3The sea saw it, and fled;
  The Jordan turned backward.
4The mountains skipped like rams,
  The hills like young sheep.
5What aileth thee O thou sea, that thou fleest?
  Thou Jordan, that thou turnest backward?
6Ye mountains, that ye skip like rams;
  Ye hills, like young sheep?
7Tremble, thou earth, at the presence of the Lord,
  At the presence of the God of Jacob;
8Who turned the rock into a pool of water,
  The flint into a fountain of waters.

Slave people, living as strangers in a land where even the language was alien to them, suddenly—explosively—break out of their imprisonment. That is reversal of fortune on a historic scale. It certainly is an occasion for wonder. Yet such overwhelming and wondrous events are exactly what transpired for the Hebrew slaves.

As we read Psalm 114, we can also understand it as describing the ultimate outcome of our own "enslavements" to the forces that oppress us and appear destined to rule us. Psalm 114 is a reflection of historic events and by extension a promise of the future liberation that can come to us, freeing us from the "Egypts" of our lives. Reversals of fortune have taken place in the past, this psalm assures us, no matter how amazing such a prospect appears to us while we are in the midst of our own experience of degradation.

Before leaving Psalm 114 we should take note of the extraordinary image with which the psalmist chose to conclude it: "Who turned the rock into a pool of water, / The flint into a fountain of waters." Why would the psalmist leave us with this particular image? Once again these verses call to mind an event described in the biblical account of the Exodus (as do references to the sea fleeing). The verses allude to when Moses spoke to a rock, or struck it, and caused it to turn into a spring of water for his parched people (Exodus 17:6 and Numbers 20:11). But there is a particular purpose for evoking those events here.

The more we reflect on this incident, the more we recognize that it constitutes its own form of reversal. What could be a clearer symbol of change than this? The rock, after all, is the symbol *par excellence* of all that is solid and changeless. In these accounts it is suddenly turned into unrestrained, gushing liquid: water, the very embodiment of mutability, flowing, moving, adapting itself to the contours of whatever contains it, and changing everything it encounters.

Nature plays an important role in Psalm 114's theme of reversal of fortune. As we reflect on this image drawn from biblical history, we find it echoing earlier verses in this psalm: "The sea saw it, and fled; / The Jordan turned backward. / The mountains skipped like rams, / The hills like young sheep." These verses also attest to more than a historical moment. The sea, the Jordan, the mountains and the hills do more than express amazement at the events of the Exodus. In their very reaction they embody reversal. Hills and mountains are not supposed to skip and jump, and seas stay in their place. What could symbolize reversal more than the psalm's description of the Jordan, which has turned backward?

Beneath these images, the psalmist has hidden the ultimate lesson of the psalm. These examples constitute nothing less than a reversal of the laws of nature, and with it the psalm directs our attention to an important reality: The God who controls—and can reverse—the laws of nature is the God who can become involved in human history. The God who can turn rocks into pools of water, cause the Jordan to run backward, and part the waters of the Red Sea is also the God who can reverse what feels like inexorable forces controlling our destinies. The God of nature and the God of history, the psalm underscores, are one. God can enter into the personal histories of each of our lives.

Reading the psalms assures us that we are not held captive on a one-way journey. Our lives, like our fates, are not sealed solid as a rock, but can be transformed. Our circumstances can be turned into life-enhancing forces—like water slaking our thirst when we are parched.

We find these same themes sounded in Psalm 68.

> [5]Sing unto God, sing praises to His name;
> Extol Him that rideth upon the skies, whose name is
>     the Lord;
> And exult ye before Him.
> [6]A father of the fatherless, and a judge of the widows,
> Is God in His holy habitation.
> [7]God maketh the solitary to dwell in a house;
> He bringeth out the prisoners into prosperity;
> The rebellious dwell but in a parched land.

⁸O God, when Thou wentest forth before Thy people,
When Thou didst march through the wilderness;
⁹The earth trembled, the heavens also dropped at the
    presence of God;
Even yon Sinai trembled at the presence of God, the God
    of Israel.

Here again, nature is invoked in a double capacity. Verse 9 recalls for us the historical moment when the Jewish people gathered at Mount Sinai to receive the Torah: "Now Mount Sinai was all in smoke, for the Lord had come down upon it in fire; the smoke rose like the smoke of a kiln, and the whole mountain trembled violently." (Exodus 19:18) At the same time, nature is depicted as having an emotional response to the wonder of this moment.

Psalm 68 makes explicit the connection between the liberation of the people who came to Sinai in the midst of their flight from slavery and the individual who knows personal enslavement and oppression. Verse 7 may be talking about the collective experience of the liberated slaves, but more immediately, it talks to all of us in times when we feel alone or imprisoned. This psalm talks not about the degradation that comes at these times, but about the joy, wonder, and amazement that overwhelms us—and spreads to all of nature—when our reversal of fortune occurs.

Psalm 68 seems to be telling us that if the liberation of an entire nation can happen (an event so profound as to make even solid mountains tremble), certainly there is hope for companionship when we feel solitary and freedom when we feel like prisoners of whatever it is that has confined us. The story of Exodus is the story of each one of us, the psalm asserts. Nature is an astonished witness (just as we saw in Psalm 114) as the imprisoned go free.

Psalms 113 and 114, which we have examined, are the first two psalms in the *Hallel,* a grouping of psalms which is incorporated into the synagogue worship service on the three "pilgrimage" festivals—*Pesach, Sukkot* and *Shavuot*—on *Chanukah,* and on *Rosh Chodesh,* the beginning of the new month. The last psalm in the *Hallel* is Psalm 118. It is an exultant and triumphant expression of the idea of the reversal of fortune.

1"O give thanks unto the Lord, for He is good,
  For His mercy endureth for ever."
2So let Israel now say,
  For His mercy endureth for ever.
3So let the house of Aaron now say,
  For His mercy endureth for ever.
4So let them now that fear the Lord say,
  For His mercy endureth for ever.
5Out of my straits I called upon the Lord;
  He answered me with great enlargement.
6The Lord is for me; I will not fear;
  What can man do unto me?
7The Lord is for me as my helper;
  And I shall gaze upon them that hate me.
8It is better to take refuge in the Lord
  Than to trust in man.
9It is better to take refuge in the Lord
  Than to trust in princes.
10All nations compass me about;
  Verily, in the name of the Lord I will cut them off.
11They compass me about, yea, they compass me about;
  Verily, in the name of the Lord I will cut them off.
12They compass me about like bees;
  They are quenched as the fire of thorns;
  Verily, in the name of the Lord I will cut them off.

¹³Thou didst thrust sore at me that I might fall;
   But the Lord helped me.
¹⁴The Lord is my strength and song;
   And He is become my salvation.
¹⁵The voice of rejoicing and salvation is in the tents of the
      righteous;
   The right hand of the Lord doth valiantly.
¹⁶The right hand of the Lord is exalted;
   The right hand of the Lord doth valiantly.
¹⁷I shall not die, but live,
   And declare the works of the Lord.
¹⁸The Lord hath chastened me sore;
   But He hath not given me over unto death.
¹⁹Open to me the gates of righteousness;
   I will enter into them, I will give thanks unto the Lord.
²⁰This is the gate of the Lord;
   The righteous shall enter into it.
²¹I will give thanks unto Thee, for Thou hast answered me,
   And art become my salvation.
²²The stone which the builders rejected
   Is become the chief corner-stone.
²³This is the Lord's doing;
   It is marvelous in our eyes.
²⁴This is the day which the Lord hath made;
   We will rejoice and be glad in it.
²⁵We beseech thee, O Lord, save now!
   We beseech Thee, O Lord, make us now to prosper!
²⁶Blessed be he that cometh in the name of the Lord;
   We bless you out of the house of the Lord.
²⁷The Lord is God, and hath given us light;
   Order the festival procession with boughs, even unto
      the horns of the altar.

²⁸Thou art my God, and I will give thanks unto Thee;
   Thou art my God, I will exalt Thee.
²⁹O give thanks unto the Lord, for He is good,
   For His mercy endureth for ever.

The language and rhythms of the psalm express a sense of rejoicing and exhilaration. Psalm 118 is clearly about the deliverance of the individual rather than the nation. It is explicitly about the protagonist—and about the reader, who cannot help but take the first person singular language of the psalm as speaking of him- or herself—overcoming adversities and prevailing over adversaries. As we read this song of deliverance, the most compelling images, and the ones on which the psalm turns, make concrete for us the idea of the reversal of fate.

¹⁰All nations compass me about;
   Verily, in the name of the Lord I will cut them off.
¹¹They compass me about, yea, they compass me about;
   Verily, in the name of the Lord I will cut them off.
¹²They compass me about like bees;
   They are quenched as the fire of thorns;
   Verily, in the name of the Lord I will cut them off.
¹³Thou didst thrust sore at me that I might fall;
   But the Lord helped me.
¹⁴The Lord is my strength and song;
   And He is become my salvation.
¹⁵The voice of rejoicing and salvation is in the tents of
      the righteous . . .

A little later in the psalm we come upon the most stirring embodiment of this theme in the powerful image of verse 22: "The stone which the builders rejected / Is become the chief corner-stone." These few words—just six in the Hebrew original—speak volumes about what it means to go from degradation to exaltation. Entire novels and dramas have been written over the millennia seeking to express what it means for a person to feel cast off and useless, only to be recognized and acclaimed as possessing value and then elevated to the very highest ranks. Yet these ideas find a most forceful expression in these six words in Psalm 118.

There are so many examples of this reversal of fortune in the Book of Psalms that we cannot explore them all. Let us take note of just a few more. In Psalm 4 we find a dramatic shift in tone and mood from the first seven verses to the last two. In the earlier verses, we read of a person in distress and agony who feels abandoned, overcome with suffering. The final verses give voice to confidence and security. The protagonist has gone through some transforming experience that has left him on wholly new terrain.

At the beginning of Psalm 6, the protagonist—the "I" of the text and the "I" who reads the text—is also suffering some terrible affliction. But between verse 8 and verse 9, it is clear that some dramatic change has occurred in the protagonist's circumstances and outlook.

Psalm 10 begins with the image of God as remote and indifferent. Verses 1–15 are filled with grim images of the anarchy and violence that can prevail in a world in which God is absent. Verses 16–18, however, reflect a very different state of affairs. Circumstances have changed dramatically. In these concluding verses, God is emphatically present, hearing the cries of the humble and seeing the plots of the wicked. God is hailed as King defending the cause of the needy. This same shift occurs in many of the psalms: in Psalm 13, between verses 5 and 6; in Psalm 22 between verses 22 and 23; in Psalm 28 between verses 5 and 6; in Psalm 31 between verses 19 and 20; in Psalm 32 between verses 6 and 7; and in so many others.

## Exploring Joseph's Reversal of Fortune

Psalm 30 contains verses that seem a fit note on which to end our exploration of the concept of reversal of fortune.

¹A Psalm; a Song at the Dedication of the House; of David
²I will extol Thee, O Lord, for Thou hast raised me up,
 And hast not suffered mine enemies to rejoice over me.
³O Lord my God,
 I cried unto Thee, and Thou didst heal me;
⁴O Lord, Thou broughtest up my soul from the nether-world;
 Thou didst keep me alive, that I should not go down to
  the pit.
⁵Sing praise unto the Lord, O ye His godly ones,
 And give thanks to His holy name.
⁶For His anger is but for a moment,
 His favour is for a life-time;
 Weeping may tarry for the night,
 But joy cometh in the morning.
⁷Now I had said in my security:
 "I shall never be moved."
⁸Thou hadst established, O Lord, in Thy favour my mountain
  as a stronghold—
 Thou didst hide Thy face; I was affrighted.
⁹Unto Thee, O Lord, did I call,
 And unto the Lord I made supplication:
¹⁰"What profit is there in my blood, when I go down to
  the pit?
 Shall the dust praise Thee? shall it declare Thy truth?
¹¹Hear, O Lord, and be gracious unto me;
 Lord, be Thou my helper."

¹²Thou didst turn for me my mourning into dancing;
   Thou didst loose my sackcloth, and gird me with gladness;
¹³So that my glory may sing praise to Thee, and not be silent;
   O Lord my God, I will give thanks unto Thee for ever.

Here, too, we can hear the rejoicing of the person saved from catastrophe.

It is exciting to come upon references to "the pit" in verses 4 and 10, for they evoke the most dramatic account of reversal of fortune in the Bible: the saga of Joseph. Joseph was the son whose arrival was so longed for by Rachel. Jacob, his father, loved Joseph more than any of Joseph's brothers because he was the child of his beloved Rachel, and he set him above the rest. For this reason, the brothers hated Joseph and plotted to rid themselves of him. They bound him and lowered him into a pit. (Genesis 37:24–28) Joseph knew what it was "to go down into the pit."

Joseph's life, like our own, is a series of reversals of fortune. In fact, his life can literally be seen as a series of downs and ups. From being above his brothers, he was lowered by them into the pit. He was hoisted back up by them only to be sold to slave traders who took him down to Egypt. In Egypt Joseph rose to become in charge of his master's house, until fate decreed that he be sent down again to a pit—prison in Egypt. In the end, he rose once more to become, in his own words, "a father to Pharaoh . . . and ruler over all the land of Egypt." (Genesis 45:8) Joseph, who knew what it was to be in the pit, saw his fortune reversed, until finally he was able to reconcile with his brothers, and reunite with his father in triumph. He ended his days having accomplished more than even he, the master of dreams, could have dreamed possible.

## Moving Our Lives from Mourning to Joy

Psalm 30 is full of triumph and gratitude, but the words that are most striking, that can give us a sense of the possibility of hope in our own lives, sing of reversal. Who cannot be moved by the promises of verses 6 and 12?

> <sup>6</sup>For His anger is but for a moment,
> His favour is for a life-time;
> Weeping may tarry for the night,
> But joy cometh in the morning.
>
> <sup>12</sup>Thou didst turn for me my mourning into dancing;
> Thou didst loose my sackcloth, and gird me with gladness . . .

The contemporary poet, David Rosenberg, beautifully captures the sense of verse 6:

> . . . cry yourself to sleep
> but when you awake
> light is all around you . . .

Each of us knows what it is to be overcome by our burdens, fears, and anxieties. They seem to have special power over us at night, or when our lives seem the darkest. But they need not take up permanent residence with us. For, as our prayer book assures us, "the world is created anew each day." Verse 12 reminds us of the chance for this daily new beginning in our lives. We can move from grief and mourning to rejoicing and gladness. We can move from the domain of death to the realm of life.

Death takes many forms. To live as a human being is to know what it is to grieve for loved ones and friends who have died. But

so much of our life involves other kinds of loss: the end of a relationship; the loss of love; the withering away of a sense of purpose
or meaning in life. Often we find ourselves mourning the death of
hopes and dreams. But unlike physical death, so much of what we
mourn can be regained, even reborn: love, hope, purpose. These
verses from Psalm 30 are the epitome of the special promise we
have examined in this chapter: reversal of fortune. Verse 12
evokes the assurance that we are capable of experiencing the most
profound reversal of all—from "death" to life renewed.

# 4

# WHEN IT FEELS LIKE
# GOD IS ABSENT

She had been a faithful servant to her mistress, discharging all of her responsibilities dutifully and with good cheer. Given the customs of her society it seemed only natural that she fulfill her mistress' command to bear her mistress' husband a son when her mistress proved unable to bear him an heir. Then, unexpectedly, given her extremely advanced years, her mistress bore her husband a son of her own. The mistress began to view her faithful servant with distrust and to treat her abusively. The mistress convinced her husband to send the servant and her child away, out into the wilderness with only a little bread and a bottle of water. Can you hear her cry out in the words of Shakespeare's grief-maddened Romeo?:

> Hence "banished" is banished from the world,
> And world's exile is death. Then "banished"
> Is death misterm'd. Calling death "banished,"
> Thou cutt'st my head off with a golden axe
> And smilest upon the stroke that murders me.
> (*Romeo and Juliet* III.3 19–23)

We learn nothing of the servant's feelings, though; she does not put them into words. Instead she endures her ordeal in virtual silence. Only when all the water in the bottle is used up, and she has placed her son under one of the desert shrubs and removed herself a distance away, saying, "Let me not look upon the death of the child," does she raise her voice and weep. (Genesis 21:16)

This is the story of Hagar, the Egyptian servant whom Sarah "gave . . . to Abraham her husband to be his wife." (Genesis 16:3) It was Hagar who first bore Abraham the son for whom he longed when Sarah was unable to conceive. Then, after Sarah gave birth to Isaac, she insisted that Abraham drive Hagar and her son Ishmael out of the household. With evident reluctance Abraham complied.

We can only imagine the emotions that must have overwhelmed Hagar during these events. The ties that linked her to Sarah were ruptured; her emotional connection with Abraham, whatever its nature, was suddenly shattered. Driven from the only home she had known all these years, she and her son faced the gravest peril, even likely death. She must have felt maternal protectiveness for Ishmael, and terror at his prospects, and her own. Alone in that wilderness, she must have felt what can only be described as abandoned.

One thousand years later, another woman, Naomi, wrestled with her own experience of abandonment (the Book of Ruth). Naomi's family came from the city of Bethlehem. Hard economic conditions in her homeland forced her, her husband, and their two sons to migrate across the Syrian-African Rift Valley to the land of Moab. Soon, in quick succession, first her husband and then both of her sons died. She was left alone in a strange land. Accompanied by one of her widowed daughters-in-law, Naomi decided she had no choice but to return to Bethlehem and throw herself on the mercy of her family.

In contrast to Hagar in the Genesis story, Naomi voiced her feelings, the sense of rage and abandonment at the circumstances that joined her and Hagar over the distance of one thousand years. For indeed they were joined, joined by finding their lives disrupted and unravelled; discovering themselves alone, without a male protector or provider; joined by the anguish of sons dead or dying. Naomi gave voice to the welter of emotions roiling within both of them:

> When they arrived in Bethlehem, the whole city buzzed with excitement over them. The women said, "Can this be Naomi (pleasant one)?"
>
> She replied, "Do not call me Naomi, call me Mara (bitter one) for the Most High has made my lot very bitter. I went out full, and the Lord has brought me back empty. Why do you call me Naomi when the Lord has dealt harshly with me—the Most High has brought misfortune upon me?" (Ruth 1:19–21)

What a powerful expression of the plight of these two women who found themselves abandoned.

## Where Is God When We Feel Alone?

Abandonment. Without expecting it, we find it running like a crimson thread through the tapestry of the biblical narrative. Deservedly or not, so many of the biblical figures find themselves alone and afraid, in an unfamiliar environment without a guide:

Adam and Eve were driven out of the garden; Cain, with that mark on his head, was sent to wander the face of the earth after he committed the first murder—and the first fratricide. How must Isaac have felt, bound atop a pyre of logs, waiting for his father to unsheathe the knife that would end his life and render him the first Hebrew human sacrifice? Later, much later, we encounter Elijah fleeing the wrath of King Ahab and Queen Jezebel, discovering himself absolutely alone and bereft in the wilderness of Sinai, desperately seeking the presence of the God who was revealed there to Moses.

This theme of abandonment and the welter of feelings that accompany it described throughout the Bible show us what a significant element this can be in the way we think about God. Certainly Jews living in the wake of the Shoah cannot fail to ask themselves the question, "Where was God?" Historian David Wyman has written a damning account of the indifference of the world to the destruction of Europe's Jews, entitled *The Abandonment of the Jews.* We could use that same phrase to reflect on the theological implications of those events as well.

In a famous statement from the period of the Shoah, the Protestant pastor Martin Niemoeller wrote about what it felt like to be among those who were initially willing to turn their backs on people endangered and needing protection, and then, ultimately, to be among those left to the mercy of the forces of destruction:

> In Germany, the Nazis first came for the Communists and
> I did not speak up because I was not a Communist. Then
> they came for the Jews, and I did not speak up because I
> was not a Jew. Then they came for the trade unionists and
> I did not speak up because I was not a trade unionist. Then

they came for the Catholics and I was a Protestant so I did
not speak up. Then they came for me . . . by that time there
was no one to speak up for anyone.

The theological corollary to this is the painful sense that in the
midst of our most dire need, there was no One there to speak up
for us—God was absent.

The question of divine abandonment does not only resonate
on the stage of great historical events. Everyone can tell of times
in their lives when they felt utterly alone. Each of us can speak
about times when the people we depended on the most simply
were not there for us, when people we hoped would stand up for
us seemed indifferent to what became of us. And times when we
tried to find strength or comfort from our faith, and we could not
stop ourselves from asking, as Naomi did, "How could God let this
happen to me?"

Being left on our own to fend for ourselves in the face of
adversity and overwhelming challenge is the stuff of nightmares.
The truth is that virtually none of us can read Hagar's and
Naomi's stories and the others without recalling times when abandonment seemed like the status of our own life. Even as we felt
deserted by our fellow human beings who were not there in the
way we needed them to be, the religious dimension of us asks no
less vehemently, *where was God in all this? Why did God not spare me,
or intercede for me? Why was God not at my side when I needed God the
most?* All of us have times when the hallmark of our religious experience is the absence of God.

The experience of God's absence has been characterized by
some modern thinkers as "the death of God." Martin Buber captures the nuances and pathos of this experience when he calls it,

in the title of his challenging book, *The Eclipse of God.* There are times in every life when God seems hidden, when the warmth and nurture we desire and need is replaced by cold darkness. At these times our prayers cannot be of thanksgiving, praise, or even petition. All that we can do is cry out, like a person separated from his or her travelling companions in a strange and vaguely threatening environment, "Where are you?"

When we are in its grip, this sense of abandonment can feel like something unique to ourselves. It is not. And it is not something that any of us should feel ashamed of. Sometimes, when we experience this feeling we ask ourselves if we are losing our faith in God or ceasing to be a religious person. Actually the opposite is true. The sense of pain or anguish at what feels like the absence of God is its own profound kind of religiousness. It is a special way of relating to God, one that bears witness to the intensity and importance of that relationship in our own lives— just as only those who love each other can feel deeply the pangs of separation. Anguish at God's separation from us is not a rejection of God, but a deeply emotional testimony to the role that God plays in our lives.

## When It Feels Like God Is Absent from Our Lives: Looking to the Psalms

Sometimes we assume that this constellation of thoughts and feelings is unique to people of the modern age. Actually, it received its most powerful expression thousands of years ago. We can look to the Book of Psalms to help us handle the feelings of abandonment we all experience at different times in our lives. Psalms puts into words beautifully and starkly what we have felt within our hearts.

Psalm 31, verse 13, captures the inner emotions of someone who feels abandoned: "I am forgotten as a dead man out of mind; I am like a useless vessel." Indeed this verse is part of a series of verses in Psalm 31 that gives powerful insight into the emotional world of someone who feels cut off from their fellow human beings and from God:

> 11 For my life is spent in sorrow, and my years in sighing;
> My strength faileth because of mine iniquity, and my
>     bones are wasted away.
> 12 Because of all mine adversaries I am become a reproach,
> Yea, unto my neighbours exceedingly, and a dread to
>     mine acquaintance;
> They that see me outside flee from me.
> 13 I am forgotten as a dead man out of mind;
> I am like a useless vessel.

We feel utterly alone. People have turned their backs on us. Even God seems uninterested in us. In these dark times, we feel ourselves forgotten, useless, even dead.

While abandonment by our fellow humans is clear and explicit in Psalm 31, abandonment by God is only implied. It is stated more explicitly and boldly elsewhere in Psalms, and we could create a powerful—and chilling—litany from individual verses of various psalms:

> 1 Why, O God, hast Thou cast us off for ever?
> Why doth Thine anger smoke against the flock of
>     Thy pasture?
> (Psalm 74:1)

¹Why standest Thou afar off, O Lord?
  Why hidest Thou Thyself in times of trouble?
  (Psalm 10:1)

²⁴Awake, why sleepest Thou, O Lord?
  Arouse Thyself, cast not off for ever.
²⁵Wherefore hidest Thou Thy face,
  And forgettest our affliction and our oppression?
²⁶For our soul is bowed down to the dust;
  Our belly cleaveth unto the earth.
²⁷Arise for our help,
  And redeem us for Thy mercy's sake.
  (Psalm 44:24–27)

¹⁰I will say unto God my Rock:
  "Why hast Thou forgotten me?
  Why go I mourning under the oppression of the enemy?"
¹¹As with a crushing in my bones, mine adversaries taunt me;
  While they say unto me all the day: "Where is thy God?"
  (Psalm 42:10–11)

During times when our lives resonate with the mood of these psalms, God seems remote and absent to us. We feel like God has forgotten all about us, or cast us off. More darkly, we fear that perhaps God even smolders with anger against us. The psalms make repeated use of the powerful image of God's face being hidden from us. Admittedly, today we tend to be uncomfortable with anthropomorphic images that speak of God in terms of human attributes. Yet this image does strike a chord in us. It feels to us that God is not merely away, but is holding back from us, hiding.

Like the face of the sun hidden by clouds, or during an eclipse, God's face feels hidden from us in our time of need.

Paradoxically, these verses from psalms bring a particular kind of comfort to us because they assure us that we are not alone in feeling cut off from God when we need God's presence. Others experience this same eclipse, the psalms remind us; people have anguished over it for thousands of years.

These verses also remind us that it is an authentic religious experience to feel cut off from God. The awareness of God's absence, as much as the awareness of God's presence, is part of what it is to experience life as a religious person.

These same feelings animate countless other psalms. We find one particularly powerful evocation of despair in Psalm 102. It begins by stating the mood of those who give voice to these words. Quickly it moves to a clear expression of the sense that even God feels far removed from us in the times of our distress.

[1]A Prayer of the afflicted, when he fainteth, and poureth out his complaint before the Lord.
[2]O Lord, hear my prayer,
  And let my cry come to unto Thee.
[3]Hide not Thy face from me in the day of my distress;
  Incline Thine ear unto me;
  In the day when I call answer me speedily.
[4]For my days are consumed like smoke,
  And my bones are burned as a hearth.
[5]My heart is smitten like grass, and withered;
  For I forget to eat my bread.
[6]By reason of the voice of my sighing
  My bones cleave to my flesh.

⁷I am like a pelican of the wilderness;
  I am become as an owl of the waste places.
⁸I watch, and am become
  Like a sparrow that is alone upon the housetop.
⁹Mine enemies taunt me all the day;
  They that are mad against me do curse by me.
¹⁰For I have eaten ashes like bread,
  And mingled my drink with weeping.
¹¹Because of Thine indignation and Thy wrath;
  For Thou hast taken me up, and cast me away.
¹²My days are like a lengthening shadow;
  And I am withered like grass.

As we read this psalm we can speculate on the circumstances from which it emerged. It resonates with overtones of the destruction of the Temple in Jerusalem in 586 B.C.E., and can readily be understood as a petition of one of the exiles from Jerusalem. The fall of the Temple and the people's exile was no less traumatic in its time than the Shoah was in our own. The people as a whole couldn't help but ask "Where is God?" in the midst of this cataclysm.

Yet the psalm talks urgently and directly to the reader on a very personal level. When we feel ourselves adrift, we can identify with the poetically compelling images of verses 7–8, 10, and 12. By reflecting on these images drawn from nature, we can experience the emotions within ourselves. They talk to what it feels like to be cast off and alone, to feel that there is no home, no secure place, in this world for us.

If you read the remainder of this psalm you will experience a powerful transition in mood and participate in the journey from hopelessness to confidence. That movement is spelled out in more personal terms in a number of other psalms.

Psalm 88 gives us a good insight into the powerful dialectic of Psalms. Clearly it is the cry of one who feels abandoned.

2O Lord, God of my salvation,
  What time I cry in the night before Thee,
3Let my prayer come before Thee,
  Incline Thine ear unto my cry.
4For my soul is sated with troubles,
  And my life draweth nigh unto the grave.
5I am counted with them that go down into the pit;
  I am become as a man that hath no help;
6Set apart among the dead,
  Like the slain that lie in the grave,
  Whom Thou rememberest no more;
  And they are cut off from Thy hand.
7Thou hast laid me in the nethermost pit,
  In dark places, in the deeps.
8Thy wrath lieth hard upon me,
  And all Thy waves Thou pressest down.
9Thou hast put mine acquaintance far from me;
  Thou hast made me an abomination unto them;
  I am shut up, and I cannot come forth.
10Mine eye languisheth by reason of affliction;
  I have called upon Thee, O Lord, every day,
  I have spread forth my hands unto Thee.
11Wilt Thou work wonders for the dead?
  Or shall the shades arise and give Thee thanks?

<sup>12</sup>Shall Thy mercy be declared in the grave?
  Or Thy faithfulness in destruction?
<sup>13</sup>Shall Thy wonders be known in the dark?
  And Thy righteousness in the land of forgetfulness?
<sup>14</sup>But as for me, unto Thee, O Lord, do I cry,
  And in the morning doth my prayer come to meet Thee.
<sup>15</sup>Lord, why castest Thou off my soul?
  Why hidest Thou Thy face from me?
<sup>16</sup>I am afflicted and at the point of death from my youth up;
  I have borne Thy terrors, I am distracted.
<sup>17</sup>Thy fierce wrath is gone over me;
  Thy terrors have cut me off.
<sup>18</sup>They came round about me like water all the day;
  They compassed me about together.
<sup>19</sup>Friend and companion hast Thou put far from me,
  And mine acquaintance into darkness.

This psalm is almost unbearably painful to read. You can feel the piercing anguish of one who feels abandoned. As we read it, we feel our way into the author's emotions. We cry out to God, pour out our troubles. And yet, what makes those troubles harder to bear is the sense that God is somehow at the root of our problems. Certainly our fellow human beings have not helped us (verses 9, 19), but could it be that God is somehow responsible for that distance? Even more darkly, the psalm suggests that God is responsible for all the misfortunes that have befallen us (verses 7–8). Indeed, the psalmist fears that it is possible that God is angry at us (verses 8, 17). This is the same fear we encountered in Psalm 74:1. Here, in Psalm 88, the psalmist speaks in very powerful images of God's wrath and terror encircling us like waters encircling a drowning person.

Running through this very dark, desperate psalm are images of death. Verses 4 and 16 suggest that death is very near. Other verses (5–7, 11–13) suggest that we have indeed already died. Of course, that is exactly how we sometimes feel when we have experienced wrenching losses—as if we have died. The psalm is almost unrelievedly dark: We find ourselves in the very grave. And yet the smallest glimmer of hope insinuates itself almost without notice, because, when the author's voice is our own, we are not only telling God our state of mind, we are also challenging God, calling for God's help in a rather oblique way. Verse 14 acknowledges that we are asking for God's help, but so do verses 11–13:

> 11 Wilt Thou work wonders for the dead?
>   Or shall the shades arise and give Thee thanks?
> 12 Shall Thy mercy be declared in the grave?
>   Or Thy faithfulness in destruction?
> 13 Shall Thy wonders be known in the dark?
>   And Thy righteousness in the land of forgetfulness?

What these verses say to God very simply is—what use am I to You if I am dead? Once our lives are truly finished, we cannot appreciate Your wonders or praise You (verse 11), we cannot acknowledge Your mercies (verse 12) or declare Your righteousness (verse 13). This idea has been put even more succinctly and directly elsewhere:

> 17 The dead cannot praise the Lord
>   Neither any that go down [to the grave] in silence.
>   (Psalm 115:17)

¹⁰What profit is there in my blood
When I go down to the pit?
Shall the dust praise You,
Shall it make known Your truth?
(Psalm 30:10)


⁶For in death there is no remembrance of You.
In the nether-world who will give You thanks?
(Psalm 6:6)


Once we recognize the undertone to these verses we can also note that they constitute the beginning of movement from out of the pit of our despair.

Here the reversal of fortune begins, for the significant thing about these feelings of alienation is not that we have them, but that we move beyond them. To move toward healing we must first acknowledge that we feel ourselves cut off, abandoned. The psalms we have read reflect an author who has done that, and help us do that as well. The next step is for us to move from a sense of God's distance to the sense that we can call on God for help. That is what the series of verses above do. They begin, timidly enough, to enlist God as a helper. God becomes involved in our situation and enrolled in our cause. After all, *what good am I to You, if I have entered the domain of death?*

We see even more dramatic movement in Psalm 22. This psalm begins on the same note of abandonment as the ones we have already examined. It evokes the same constellation of anguish, fear, and despair. Yet this psalm goes further than Psalm 88 in crying out to God to end the eclipse of God's face and come to our help.

Before we look at Psalm 22, it should be noted that it comes freighted with additional baggage in the history of religion. Different religious traditions have different answers to the question of what this psalm is about.

Christian tradition tends to read this psalm following a style of reading called *typology*—reading Hebrew scriptures in the light of the Gospel events. Thus, Christian reading sees Psalm 22 as a foreshadowing of the Passion of Jesus. In many of its images Christian interpreters have seen an anticipation of events of the crucifixion. Verse 2 has gained a special place in Christian tradition as the words Jesus spoke on the cross (Matthew 27:46; Mark 15:34).

Some Jewish interpreters see this cry for help as reflecting events in the life of David when he was being pursued by King Saul. Others find it a collective expression of distress on the part of the entire Jewish people at the time of some national calamity. This interpretation is sustained by verses 5 and 6. The medieval commentator David Qimhi suggested that this psalm was the outpouring of the Jewish people during the threat to their lives by Haman, as described in *K'tuvim* in the Book of Esther.

Whatever its origins and however we understand its historical associations, this psalm can most powerfully be read as the outpouring of its author's personal despair. As we read it we can trace the lines of our own emotions in it. At the beginning we feel abandoned and utterly alone. We then move toward understanding that we can ask for help and hope for deliverance:

²My God, my God, why hast Thou forsaken me,
   And art far from my help at the words of my cry?

³O my God, I call by day, but Thou answerest not;

And at night, and there is no surcease for me.

⁴Yet Thou art holy,

O Thou that art enthroned upon the praises of Israel.

⁵In Thee did our fathers trust;

They trusted, and Thou didst deliver them.

⁶Unto Thee they cried, and escaped;

In Thee did they trust, and were not ashamed.

⁷But I am a worm, and no man;

A reproach of men, and despised of the people.

⁸All they that see me laugh me to scorn;

They shoot out the lip, they shake the head:

⁹"Let him commit himself unto the Lord! let Him rescue him;

Let Him deliver him, seeing He delighteth in him."

¹⁰For Thou art He that took me out of the womb;

Thou madest me trust when I was upon my mother's
breasts.

¹¹Upon Thee I have been cast from my birth;

Thou art my God from my mother's womb.

¹²Be not far from me; for trouble is near;

For there is none to help.

¹³Many bulls have encompassed me;

Strong bulls of Bashan have beset me round.

¹⁴They open wide their mouth against me,

As a ravening and a roaring lion.

¹⁵I am poured out like water,

And all my bones are out of joint;

My heart is become like wax;

It is melted in mine inmost parts.

¹⁶My strength is dried up like a potsherd;

And my tongue cleaveth to my throat;

And Thou layest me in the dust of death.

¹⁷For dogs have encompassed me;

A company of evil-doers have inclosed me;

Like a lion, they are at my hands and my feet.

¹⁸I may count all my bones;

They look and gloat over me.

¹⁹They part my garments among them,

And for my vesture do they cast lots.

²⁰But Thou, O Lord, be not far off;

O Thou my strength, hasten to help me.

²¹Deliver my soul from the sword;

Mine only one from the power of the dog.

²²Save me from the lion's mouth;

Yea, from the horns of the wild-oxen do Thou answer me.

²³I will declare Thy name unto my brethren;

In the midst of the congregation will I praise Thee:

²⁴"Ye that fear the Lord, praise Him;

All ye the seed of Jacob, glorify Him;

And stand in awe of Him, all ye the seed of Israel.

²⁵For He hath not despised nor abhorred the lowliness of

the poor;

Neither hath He hid His face from him;

But when he cried unto Him, He heard."

²⁶From Thee cometh my praise in the great congregation;

I will pay my vows before them that fear Him.

²⁷Let the humble eat and be satisfied;

Let them praise the Lord that seek after Him;

May your heart be quickened for ever!
<sup>28</sup>All the ends of the earth shall remember and turn unto
    the Lord;
And all the kindreds of the nations shall worship before Thee.
<sup>29</sup>For the kingdom is the Lord's
And He is the ruler over the nations.
<sup>30</sup>All the fat ones of the earth shall eat and worship;
All they that go down to the dust shall kneel before Him,
Even he that cannot keep his soul alive.
<sup>31</sup>A seed shall serve Him;
It shall be told of the Lord unto the next generation.
<sup>32</sup>They shall come and shall declare His righteousness
Unto a people that shall be born, that He hath done it.

Verse 2 describes the feeling of abandonment by God as starkly as can be imagined. God has left us, does not answer us or give us comfort (verse 3). The psalm captures what we feel about ourselves during despair in a wonderfully evocative image: "But I am a worm, and no man; / A reproach of men, and despised of the people." In another series of terrifying images it describes how our life feels to us:

<sup>15</sup>I am poured out like water,
And all my bones are out of joint;
My heart is become like wax;
It is melted in mine inmost parts.
<sup>16</sup>My strength is dried up like a potsherd;
And my tongue cleaveth to my throat;
And Thou layest me in the dust of death.

<sup>17</sup>For dogs have encompassed me;

A company of evil-doers have inclosed me;

Like a lion, they are at my hands and my feet.

<sup>18</sup>I may count all my bones;

They look and gloat over me.

The references to dogs and lions in these verses remind us of the rich poetic quality of this psalm. Psalm 22 contains a veritable bestiary: worms, bulls, lions, dogs, and oxen populate this psalm. Similarly, the references to tongue and throat call to mind that the psalm is also rich in anatomical allusions, mentioning lips, head, stomach, breasts, womb, mouth, bones, heart, inmost parts, tongue, throat, hands, and feet. The images in this psalm are rich and dense.

In verse 16 we again hear the imagery of death that we noted in our discussion of Psalm 88. But Psalm 22 does not stay in the pit. It differs from Psalm 88 in that is makes a powerful appeal for God's help. The psalmist describes the ostracism we feel from our fellow human beings (verses 8–9) when we are feeling abandoned, but that reference serves as a transition to a testimony to the psalmist's confidence in God (verses 10–11). It was, the psalmist reminds us, God who formed us and God who has been present for us from the time of our conception. If those who are abandoning us say "let Him rescue him" (verse 9), the psalmist turns their words around and calls on God to turn their words of scorn into divine deeds of salvation.

The author of Psalm 22 is not averse to asking God for help (verses 12, 20–22). The sense of utter abandonment at the beginning of the psalm gives way to hope of divine aid. The psalmist marks out the road that each of us can travel to move beyond our sense of abandonment and alienation to a renewed sense of God's presence and potential for partnership. That impassioned cry for God's help can become our own as we read this psalm and others like it. It can become our most sincere prayer in our darkest times.

After the plea for help in verses 20–22, this psalm takes a dramatic turn. The concluding verses—23–32—are words not of petition but of praise, as if the hoped-for act of rescue had taken place. Somewhere between verse 22 and 23 the psalmist experiences what all of us can hope for: deliverance from whatever it is that afflicts us. The author has not only been lifted out of the pit, but also has been restored to human community (verse 26).

The psalm holds out the hope that we can move beyond our travails and beyond the burden of human isolation. In its conclusion it affirms for us that we can also regain the intimacy with God, the absence of which was the emblem of the beginning of this psalm. The very last words of Psalm 22 are words of powerful affirmation—"[God] hath done it."

Psalm 22 embodies the journey all of us can make from alienation to affirmation, from the depths of the pit to the heights of promises fulfilled. As we read Psalm 22 we are privileged not merely to hear about the journey, but to experience it within ourselves.

Having travelled the road out of the pit in Psalm 22, we can better understand the dramatic movement in a very similar psalm, the brief and compellingly crafted Psalm 13.

> [2] How long, O Lord, wilt Thou forget me for ever?
>   How long wilt Thou hide Thy face from me?
> [3] How long shall I take counsel in my soul,
>   Having sorrow in my heart by day?
>   How long shall mine enemy be exalted over me?

⁴Behold Thou, and answer me, O Lord my God;

  Lighten mine eyes, lest I sleep the sleep of death;

⁵Lest mine enemy say: "I have prevailed against him";

  Lest mine adversaries rejoice when I am moved.

⁶But as for me, in Thy mercy do I trust;

  My heart shall rejoice in Thy salvation.

  I will sing unto the Lord,

  Because He hath dealt bountifully with me.

Here we find many of the same elements with which we have become familiar. The psalm begins by giving voice to a sense of God's remoteness (verses 2–3). Quickly it moves to a plea for God to respond (verses 4–5). As in earlier psalms, we hear the author compare feelings of despair to death itself (verse 4). In this psalm, the dramatic transition takes place between verses 5 and 6. At the conclusion of the psalm, the author speaks of God's kindness and saving actions, and sings of having trust in God's mercy. In these compact verses we read of the journey each of us can make. When we are at the earliest stages of the journey, feeling ourselves cut off and in the pit, reading of the movement in this psalm can be experienced as a promise of hope. The very brevity of this composition gives it a special power and usefulness in our lives.

Having begun this chapter with accounts of the lives of Hagar and Naomi, it seems only fitting at this point to look at the conclusion of those narratives. Just as Hagar and Naomi were similar in their travails, the conclusions of their stories take remarkably similar turns. Only after each woman has been able to give voice in her respective way to their feelings of distress and abandonment are they able to take the steps that will carry them through their alienation to fulfillment.

## Whatever Happened to Hagar and Naomi?

After Hagar has "lifted up her voice and wept" God appears to her with words of comfort and assurance. Rather than becoming a bereaved mother as she fears she will, she has a remarkable encounter with God. God appears to Hagar and addresses her directly. God's revelation to Hagar begins with the words "What ails you, Hagar?" We have encountered this same phrase before in Psalm 114:5, where it celebrates an unexpected and remarkable reversal of fortune. So, too, is Hagar's fate to be diametrically changed:

> And God heard the voice of the lad. An angel of God called to Hagar from out of the heavens and said to her, "What ails you, Hagar? Do not fear, for God has heard the voice of the lad where he is. Arise, lift up the lad, hold him fast with your hand, for I will make of him a great nation." And God caused her eyes to open and she saw a well of water. She went to it and filled the bottle with water and she caused the lad to drink. And God was with the lad and he grew up and he lived in the wilderness and became a mighty archer. He lived in the wilderness of Paran. And his mother took a wife for him from the land of Egypt.
>
> (Genesis 21:17–21)

The last verse of this account is more than an incidental domestic detail. Among many ancient peoples—and in many tribal societies today—the mother of the male head of the clan was a person of real authority. Overseeing all arrangements of the household, she was served and obeyed by her daughters-in-law. In choosing a fellow countryman—can we conjecture perhaps even a relative?—Hagar ensures that the woman who is to do her bidding will be one who is closely allied with her.

With the introduction of a wife for Ishmael, we see the beginning of the fulfillment of the divine covenant with him as well. This wife represents the promise of a child, and that first (male) heir is the necessary precondition to Ishmael becoming the ancestor of "a great nation." At the end of this account Hagar is on the brink of becoming the progenitor of an entire people. She will know domestic status and a nation of descendants.

As for Naomi, the outcome of her story is compellingly similar and no less marvelous. Once she has expressed her anger and feelings of alienation, she is able to undertake actions that will result in her being delivered from that condition. Through an indirect route, Naomi, too, finds herself joyously fulfilled and assured of her immortality through her descendants.

At the end of her story, Naomi is once again in the presence of a "Greek chorus" of the women of her village. Naomi, who had complained of coming home empty, stands with her arms full. As the village women address her in the final verses of the Book of Ruth, it would hardly occur to anyone to refer to her as *Mara* (bitterness). Her story concludes with a scene of emotional fullness:

> So Boaz married Ruth; she became his wife, and he cohabited with her. The Lord let her conceive, and she bore a son. And the women said to Naomi, "Blessed be the Lord, who has not withheld a redeemer from you today! May his name be perpetuated in Israel! He will renew your life and sustain your old age; for he is born of your daughter-in-law, who loves you and is better to you than seven sons."

Naomi took the child and held it to her bosom. She became its foster mother, and the women neighbors gave him a name, saying, "A son is born to Naomi!" They named him Obed; he was the father of Jesse, father of David.

(Ruth 4:13–17)

Under the law of the society in which Naomi lived, the so-called law of Levirate marriage (Deuteronomy 25:5–7), when a man died childless, his brother or near kinsman was obligated to marry his widow. The first child of that union was considered the child of the woman's first husband. In this story, Boaz fulfilled the role of near kinsman, and the first child born to him and Ruth was legally regarded as the child of Naomi's dead son. In every sense this child, Obed, was considered Naomi's grandchild. Thus it was her descendant, David—to whom tradition ascribes the composition of these very psalms—who would establish the great royal dynasty, and David's line—and Naomi's—from which the Messiah, the great hoped-for redeemer of the people, will come. Quite a wondrous fullness, indeed, for a woman who felt abandoned by God and reduced to coming home empty and in bitterness.

Truly, like the midwives in the story of the Exodus (Exodus 1:20), God blesses Hagar and Naomi by "making them houses." The stories of Hagar and Naomi make clear the sense of this otherwise enigmatic phrase. They are given households to rejoice in, households to nurture and protect them in their old age. They become matriarchs of clans, ancestors of nations. Both move from the terror of being abandoned and bereft to national immortality.

## Estrangement Can Be Surmounted

Each of the psalms that we have shared in this chapter serves as a reminder that we human beings can have times when we experience the most profound alienation from one another. We have times, as well, when it feels like even God has abandoned us. The frequency of this theme in psalms reminds us that such feelings are not beyond the realm of normal. From a religious perspective, they are also not suspect or heretical. To experience these times of separation from God is part of what it is to be a person of faith.

The healing power of these psalms comes through the assurance that feelings of estrangement can be surmounted. The psalmist has—and we can—move from feeling abandoned to a willingness to cry out for help. In the act of reaching out for help comes a renewed awareness of God's nearness. It is only a brief step from that recognition to being able to give thanks to God for the help we have received and to utter words of affirmation and confidence. The trajectory of the psalms can be our own: From feeling radically isolated, we, too can come to experience again the assurance that we are never alone.

# 5

*O God, Please Heal*

# IN THE FACE OF SICKNESS

An unexpected incident in the midst of the vast panorama of the Exodus gives us a chance to see Moses in very human terms—and reminds us that even when caught up in great world-shaping events, people cannot escape dealing with the limitations and concerns that are part of the reality of what it means to be a human being.

With all the demands of leading his people through the wilderness, Moses was called upon to put aside his roles of prophet, law-giver, and teacher to act in the more domestic, familial capacity of distraught brother. His sister Miriam, whether as a result of sibling rivalry or some sort of internecine power struggle, had humiliated Moses. As punishment she was stricken with a grave, perhaps even life-threatening illness. Moses had to take it upon himself to act on her behalf.

Moses, who was accustomed to bringing important concerns of the people to God's attention, now came before God to appeal for the restoration of his sister's health. Moses' words in this situation were noteworthy: It is one of the few times in the Torah we encounter a statement that can be characterized as a prayer.

Though elsewhere in the Torah Moses was able to express himself in elaborate, even eloquent terms, here he is able to utter just five simple words. We cannot help but be struck by the incantation-like quality of his brief but forceful declaration, *el na refa na la*— "O God, please God, heal her." (Numbers 12:13)

The life of the community came to a halt until it was clear that Moses' intercession had been effective. In time Miriam was restored to health and to her role among the people. More than its historical ramifications, Moses' actions remind us of his humanity, and of what it means for each of us to be human. The illness of his sister took precedence over everything else in his life—even his responsibility to move the Jewish people forward.

There is a story in the second book of Kings that begins on a note of such everyday naturalness that it strikes us as familiar. While the rest of the story is dramatic, and its ultimate denouement miraculous, its opening images are so close to our lives that surely we recognize them as the commonplace stuff of the human experience:

> The child grew up. One day, he went out to his father among the reapers. Suddenly he cried to his father, "Oh, my head, my head!" He said to a servant, "Carry him to his mother."                    (2 Kings 4:18–19)

Sickness erupting in the midst of our usual routine—what could be more true to life?

In the Buddhist tradition, sacred lore has it that Siddhartha Gautama (who would become the Buddha, the "enlightened one") was sheltered as a child and young man by his father. The reason for this was that the father, who was the ruler of his kingdom, wanted Gautama to succeed him on the throne. But the royal sages had warned him at his son's birth that the boy would renounce all worldly pursuits and become an all-knowing seer unless he was protected from seeing the three cardinal realities of the human condition: death, old age, and sickness. The sight of these conditions would cause Gautama to renounce the throne and take up the career that he ultimately did, in fact, assume. In this story, the Buddhist tradition teaches not only about the life of its founder, but also about how it views the fundamental circumstances of human life. Sickness, old age, and death are the very stuff of our experience.

Jewish tradition, too, recognizes illness, and its attendant emotional conditions, as part of what all human beings experience on their journey through life. Illness is an inescapable part of what it means to be human. As one rabbi expresses it, "No person in life is free from pain" (Yalkut Shimoni to Ekeb 850).

Jewish tradition has a deep respect for the wonder of the human body, and an awareness of its fragility. That the body itself is to be respected and taken care of is virtually an article of faith.

> A person should see to it that the body is kept healthy and strong, in order that one may be upright to know the Lord. For it is impossible to understand and comprehend the wisdom (of the world) when one is hungry and ailing or if one's limbs ache. . . . Since when the body is healthy and sound, one walks in the way of the Lord, it being impossible to understand or know anything of the knowledge of the Creator when one is sick, it is obligatory upon people to avoid things that are detrimental to the body and acclimate themselves to things that heal and fortify it.
>
> (*Mishneh Torah*, Hilkhot Deot 3:3, 4:23)

This same awareness of our body's fragility is reflected in a prayer that traditional Jewish practice would have us recite at the beginning of each day:

Blessed are You, O Lord our God, ruler of the universe, who has fashioned human beings in wisdom—creating in us orifices and apertures. It is well known before the throne of Your glory that if even one of these were to be sundered or if even one of them were to be stopped up, it would not be possible to continue to exist—or to stand before You. Blessed are You, O Lord, Healer of all flesh, who works wondrously.

This prayer expresses itself somewhat elliptically, but is nonetheless direct in an unexpectedly earthy way. It tells us that our bodies are veritable miracles, amazingly intricate and overwhelmingly delicate. Should any part of them not function properly—should our kidneys and bowels, for instance, not be able to eliminate our bodily waste—we would be rendered unable to pursue our human calling, and to go on living. We give thanks when our bodies function properly even in the most apparently mundane matters.

To live a human life is, in part, to be defined by our bodies. When they work properly, our lives feel that much easier. But there are times in everybody's life when we experience the limitations of our bodies, or when they fail us outright. As we grow in human experience—and in wisdom—we recognize, and ultimately accept, our physical fragility and illness as facts of the human condition. Still when we or somebody close to us are in the midst of illness, we need some place to turn to help us deal with it. It is often at such moments that people turn to religion.

## Drawing on Spiritual Resources for Healing

Historically many societies have used religion as a means of coping directly with illness—as a cure for disease. This is still the case in some communities today, although more commonly we turn to science and medicine to help us address illness. But increasingly we recognize that even as we seek a physical cure, we still have need for a spiritual resource to help us face the fact of our illness and to deal with the emotions it arouses in us.

There is much in the Jewish tradition that speaks of God as the source of healing. At times we find these references comforting, and at other times they make us uncomfortable. The modern temperament is disconcerted when it reads citations that concretely depict God as affecting actual recovery from illness. We might more comfortably choose to understand such readings as figuratively talking about God as the author of all that promotes our recovery, the source of all the processes—including scientific discovery and the medical attention we are receiving—that result in our cure.

It is significant that the Hebrew word *rofeh,* which is used to call God "healer," is also the word for physician, the human agent for treating disease and cure. God is the ultimate *rofeh,* the source of all that contributes to our recovery. One seventeenth-century physician, Ambroise Paré, put it very succinctly: "I dressed his wounds, and God healed him." (Benjamin Franklin put it more sardonically: "God heals and the doctor collects the fees.") Seeing our own drama—our struggle with illness and movement to wholeness—in spiritual terms is a religiously authentic posture, and, as current scientific studies now tell us, an important part of our recovery.

There is a brief but compelling episode in the Book of Isaiah (see also 2 Kings 20:1–6) that focuses our attention on the religious component of healing.

> In those days Hezekiah fell dangerously ill. The prophet Isaiah son of Amoz came and said to him, "Thus said the Lord: Set your affairs in order, for you are going to die; you

will not get well." Thereupon Hezekiah turned his face to
the wall and prayed to the Lord. "Please, O Lord," he
said, "remember how I have walked before You sincerely
and wholeheartedly, and have done what is pleasing to
You." And Hezekiah wept profusely. Then the word of the
Lord came to Isaiah: "Go and tell Hezekiah: Thus said
the Lord, the God of your father David: I have heard your
prayer, I have seen your tears. I hereby add fifteen years
to your life."                                    (Isaiah 38:1–5)

Hezekiah prayed to God for recovery, and God responded. Every
person can pray for recovery—for themselves and for their dear
ones.

In the Jewish liturgy, God is frequently invoked as *rofeh*. The
central prayer of the worship service, called *T'fillah* ("the prayer"),
is made up of nineteen separate benedictions. The eighth of
these says:

Heal us O Lord, and we shall be healed; save us and we
shall be saved. For You are our glory. Grant complete healing to all our wounds, for You O Great Ruler, are a faithful
and compassionate healer. Blessed are You O Lord, healer
of the sick of Your people Israel.

The same identification of God as healer occurs as well in the
second of these benedictions. There we extol God who "lifts up
the fallen, heals the sick, frees the captive, and keeps faith with
those who sleep in the dust."

Many people do not know that the traditional Jewish worship
service includes a prayer to be recited on behalf of people who are
ill:

May it be Your will O Lord, our God and the God of our ancestors, to send quickly complete healing from on high—healing of the soul and healing of the body to __*(Name of Person)*__ who is sick in the midst of all the others of the sick of Israel.

A similar prayer may be recited by the sick person on their own behalf. Tradition also encourages us to offer a prayer when we have recovered from illness. One modern version of such a prayer on healing reads:

O God, great, mighty and revered, in the abundance of Thy loving kindness I come before Thee to render thanks for all the benefits Thou hast bestowed upon me. In my distress I called upon Thee and Thou didst answer me; from my bed of pain I cried unto Thee and Thou didst hear the voice of my supplication. . . . Blessed art Thou, the faithful Physician of all flesh.

O God, merciful and gracious who dispensest kindness to the undeserving, I am indeed unworthy of all the mercies Thou hast hitherto shewn unto me. O purify my heart that I may be fitted to walk in the way of the upright before Thee; and continue thy help unto thy servant. Restore me to perfect health, and with bodily vigour bless Thou me.

(*Daily Prayer Book*, Joseph H. Hertz,
Chief Rabbi of the British Empire, p. 1003)

## Using the Psalms to Move from Sickness to Health

It is against this background that we can understand the way Jewish tradition has made use of the Book of Psalms as a resource in coping with illness. For those who took recourse to the magical use of psalms, *Shimush Tehillim* prescribed: Psalm 84 against sickness; Psalm 89 for the effects of sickness; Psalm 18 for all manner of sickness; Psalm 33 for epidemics; Psalms 67 and 107 for continuous fever; Psalm 49 for fever; Psalm 3 for headaches and shoulder pains; Psalm 6 for diseases of the eyes; Psalm 119 for a number of specific diseases including eye, spleen, and kidney infections, earaches, and weakness in the feet; Psalm 141 for heart disease; Psalm 142 for lumbago; Psalm 143 for arm pains; and Psalm 144 for an injured hand. Reading these psalms from a literal perspective, it is impossible to find any connection between the content of the psalms and the maladies against which they were marshaled as cure.

Elsewhere in Jewish tradition it has become *minhag* (customary practice) to read a specific selection from Psalms on behalf of a person who was gravely ill. According to this custom, we read Psalms 90–108, 20, 38, 41, 86, and 118. These are accompanied by selected verses from Psalm 119, which begin with the letters of the name of the ill person, and those verses from Psalm 119 that start with the letters that form the phrase *Kera Satan* (root out Satan). While elements of this custom work similarly to the more "magical" approach we noted in *Shimush Tehillim,* there is also more attentiveness to the content of the psalms, which we may find more useful for our own needs.

Not all of the psalms in this formula speak to the issues of sickness and healing, but a number of them offer important resources with which to address our concerns. Psalm 102 talks to the general issue of affliction and suffering. Psalms 38, 41:4–5, and 103:3 speak directly about sickness and healing. Psalms 90 and 103:13–16 raise the profound issue of human mortality and finitude, and put the reality of our illness in a significant context—one that can bring its own kind of comfort, if not cure.

Psalm 86 is a cry for help, while Psalm 107:6, 13, 19, and 28, and Psalm 20:2 assure us of God's absolute rule and attentiveness to the cries of all who call out to God. Psalm 91:11–12 is a powerful expression of God's protectiveness, so much so that the psalm is identified as a "Psalm of Protection." Finally, as we have noted elsewhere, Psalm 118 is an exultant expression of thanksgiving to God for acts of salvation, and a powerful testimony to precisely what we wish for someone who is in the midst of sickness: reversal of fortune—in this context, restoration to health.

The effect of reading this entire selection is to fix our minds on the higher issues involved in the sickness of our dear one and to leave the lessons of these particular psalms and verses imprinted on our minds. Not intended as a "cure," the reading of these psalms offers a spiritual resource to help cope with the difficult situation before us.

It is in this spirit that we can look at some of the psalms cited in this customary formula, along with several others that can be of help to us when we, or someone close to us, is confronting illness. They give voice to our anxiety and express our hope for recovery. Above all, they help us come to understand that our hope lies in a power beyond ourselves.

Before we turn to the individual readings, it should be acknowledged that many of the psalms were employed in a worldview that regarded illness as a punishment for sin. This causal relationship between suffering and wrongdoing was repudiated in the Bible (the Book of Job), and we do not have to accept the connection between sickness and sin to find meaning in the psalms. Even disconnected from that ideology, the psalms speak compellingly to the anguish of people facing illness or grateful to be restored to health.

As we have seen, the idea of God as healer is mentioned in a number of psalms, including several of those in the customary formula. Psalm 103 is an expansive hymn of praise, rejoicing in God's graciousness to the people as a whole and to individuals. It is considered one of the most exultant psalms in the entire collection:

> [1]Bless the Lord, O my soul;
> And all that is within me, bless His holy name.
> [2]Bless the Lord, O my soul,
> And forget not all His benefits;
> [3]Who forgiveth all thine iniquity;
> Who healeth all thy diseases;
> [4]Who redeemeth thy life from the pit;
> Who encompasseth thee with loving kindness and
>     tender mercies;
> [5]Who satisfieth thine old age with good things;
> So that thy youth is renewed like the eagle.
> [6]The Lord executeth righteousness,
> And acts of justice for all that are oppressed.
> [7]He made known His ways unto Moses,
> His doings unto the children of Israel.
> [8]The Lord is full of compassion and gracious,
> Slow to anger, and plenteous in mercy.
> [9]He will not always contend;
> Neither will He keep His anger for ever.
> [10]He hath not dealt with us after our sins,
> Nor requited us according to our iniquities.
> [11]For as the heaven is high above the earth,
> So great is His mercy toward them that fear Him.
> [12]As far as the east is from the west,
> So far hath He removed our transgressions from us.
> [13]Like as a father hath compassion upon his children,
> So hath the Lord compassion upon them that fear Him.
> [14]For He knoweth our frame;

He remembereth that we are dust.

15 As for man, his days are as grass;

As a flower of the field, so he flourisheth.

16 For the wind passeth over it, and it is gone;

And the place thereof knoweth it no more.

17 But the mercy of the Lord is from everlasting to everlasting

upon them that fear Him,

And His righteousness unto children's children;

18 To such as keep His covenant,

And to those that remember His precepts to do them.

19 The Lord hath established His throne in the heavens;

And His kingdom ruleth over all.

20 Bless the Lord, ye angels of His,

Ye mighty in strength, that fulfill His word.

21 Bless the Lord, all ye His hosts;

Ye ministers of His, that do His pleasure.

22 Bless the Lord, all ye His works,

In all places of His dominion;

Bless the Lord, O my soul.

Of particular interest to us here is verse 3, which praises God explicitly as a healer of diseases. God as healer is mentioned here in the context of God redeeming us from all manner of misfortunes and restoring people to well-being. The gratitude and delight of these verses is straightforward and self-evident. It talks of a God who is responsible for our recovery. By pairing God as healer with God as forgiver of iniquity, verse 3 may be affirming the ideology that links sickness to sin, but the post-Job reader does not have to accept that connection to find meaning in this verse.

As noted earlier, several later verses of this psalm—13–16— touch on another aspect of illness. Many of the psalms have the effect of reconciling us with our mortality. If, after all, our "days are as grass," then illness is part of our human estate. Such an understanding does not create a physical cure; but in helping us recognize our fundamental reality, it does help us come to terms with our situation, and perhaps even make peace with it. Though very different from the focus on healing in verse 3, this understanding can at times be a great comfort in the face of illness.

Another Psalm cited in the customary formula is Psalm 41.

2 Happy is he that considereth the poor;
   The Lord will deliver him in the day of evil.
3 The Lord preserve him, and keep him alive, let him be called
      happy in the land;
   And deliver not Thou him unto the greed of his enemies.
4 The Lord support him upon the bed of illness;
   Mayest Thou turn all his lying down in his sickness.
5 As for me, I said: "O Lord, be gracious unto me;
   Heal my soul; for I have sinned against Thee."
6 Mine enemies speak evil of me:
   "When shall he die, and his name perish?"
7 And if one come to see me, he speaketh falsehood;
   His heart gathereth iniquity to itself;
   When he goeth abroad, he speaketh of it.
8 All that hate me whisper together against me,
   Against me do they devise my hurt:
9 "An evil thing cleaveth fast unto him;
   And now that he lieth, he shall rise up no more."
10 Yea, mine own familiar friend, in whom I trusted,
      who did eat of my bread,
   Hath lifted up his heel against me.
11 But Thou, O Lord, be gracious unto me, and raise me up,
   That I may requite them.
12 By this I know that Thou delightest in me,

That mine enemy doth not triumph over me.
¹³And as for me, Thou upholdest me because of mine
    integrity,
And settest me before Thy face for ever.
¹⁴Blessed be the Lord, the God of Israel,
From Everlasting and to everlasting.
Amen, and Amen.

Again, illness is regarded as punishment for sinful actions (verses 5, 9), but here, too, we can read the psalm with benefit by disconnecting from that ideology. This psalm seems to reflect a particular circumstance. The psalmist is agitated not so much by the illness itself as by the fact that the author's enemies gloat over the author's misfortune (verses 6–9). The psalmist seems to have the preoccupation with enemies that we encounter in numerous other psalms, which we will discuss elsewhere. Even worse than the gloating of enemies, a once-trusted friend has deserted the author (verse 10). The particularity of these circumstances has led numerous traditional commentators to place this psalm in the context of King David's life, linking it to some episode in which he is described as being both ill and betrayed by a confidant. Unfortunately for this enterprise, no such incident is recorded in the chronicles of David's career. This may, in the end, be beside the point. Whoever the author is, at first reading it appears that these social realities are more pressing for the author than the actual disease.

However, several other ways of reading the text make it more pertinent to our own experience. First, we can understand these verses in a metaphorical sense. It may be that the enemies in verses 6–9 and in verse 12 are the illness itself. In that context, the once-trusted friend who has betrayed the author in verse 10 can be seen as the author's own body. Certainly all of us have experienced the feeling that our bodies have let us down, have become something that we have to contend with, even struggle against. In such a reading the true focus of our concern would not be external enemies, but the ravages of illness and the hope for recovery.

There is another reading of Psalm 41 that similarly directs our attention to the fact of disease and the hope for recovery. If we locate the dramatic turning point of the psalm between verses 10 and 11, the emphasis on enemies, and particularly on the unfaithful friend, might be seen as serving another rhetorical strategy. In such a reading the "But Thou" of verse 11 becomes the essential argument of the psalm. The author's enemies—especially the friend who has proven unreliable—serve as a contrast to God, who is gracious (verses 5, 11), faithful, and trustworthy.

The verb *betach* (trust), which the psalmist uses to describe the relationship with the false friend, is used repeatedly in the Book of Psalms to depict the trust we can have in God. Unlike the enemies who wish the psalmist ill, or the unfaithful friend, God can be counted on to "raise me up" (verse 11). From where does the author need to be raised up if not the "bed of illness" (verse 4), upon which we find the author when the psalm begins? In this reading the true subject of the psalm is illness and the psalmist's recognition of needing God's help to overcome it. Seen in this light, the psalm becomes for us a carefully constructed appeal to evoke God's concern and assistance. The psalm ends on a note of confidence that this will, in fact, take place; the author will be "upheld" (verse 13) and set before God forever. In these readings of Psalm 41, it becomes an exultant song about sickness, divine assistance, and recovery.

Another of the psalms in the formula, Psalm 107, is a reflection on different aspects of God's mercy.

¹"O give thanks unto the Lord, for He is good,
  For His mercy endureth for ever."
²So let the redeemed of the Lord say,
  Whom He hath redeemed from the hand of the adversary;
³And gathered them out of the lands
  From the east and from the west,
  From the north and from the south.
⁴They wandered in the wilderness in a desert way;
  They found no city of habitation.
⁵Hungry and thirsty,
  Their soul fainted in them.
⁶Then they cried unto the Lord in their trouble,
  And He delivered them out of their distresses.
⁷And He led them by a straight way,
  That they might go to a city of habitation.
⁸Let them give thanks unto the Lord for His mercy,
  And for His wonderful works to the children of men!
⁹For He hath satisfied the longing soul,
  And the hungry soul He hath filled with good.
¹⁰Such as sat in darkness and in the shadow of death,
  Being bound in affliction and iron—
¹¹Because they rebelled against the words of God,
  And contemned the counsel of the Most High.
¹²Therefore He humbled their heart with travail,
  They stumbled, and there was none to help—
¹³They cried unto the Lord in their trouble,
  And He saved them out of their distresses.
¹⁴He brought them out of darkness and the shadow of
    death,
  And broke their bands in sunder.
¹⁵Let them give thanks unto the Lord for His mercy,
  And for His wonderful works to the children of men!

<sup>16</sup>For He hath broken the gates of brass,
   And cut the bars of iron in sunder.
<sup>17</sup>Crazed because of the way of their transgression,
   And afflicted because of their iniquities—
<sup>18</sup>Their soul abhorred all manner of food,
   And they drew near unto the gates of death—
<sup>19</sup>They cried unto the Lord in their trouble,
   And He saved them out of their distresses;
<sup>20</sup>He sent His word, and healed them,
   And delivered them from their graves.
<sup>21</sup>Let them give thanks unto the Lord for His mercy,
   And for His wonderful works to the children of men!
<sup>22</sup>And let them offer the sacrifices of thanksgiving,
   And declare His works with singing.
<sup>23</sup>They that go down to the sea in ships,
   That do business in great waters—
<sup>24</sup>These saw the works of the Lord,
   And His wonders in the deep;
<sup>25</sup>For He commanded, and raised the stormy wind,
   Which lifted up the waves thereof;
<sup>26</sup>They mounted up to the heaven, they went down to
      the deeps;
   Their soul melted away because of trouble;
<sup>27</sup>They reeled to and fro, and staggered like a drunken
      man,
   And all their wisdom was swallowed up—
<sup>28</sup>They cried unto the Lord in their trouble,
   And He brought them out of their distresses.
<sup>29</sup>He made the storm a calm,
   So that the waves thereof were still.
<sup>30</sup>Then were they glad because they were quiet,
   And He led them unto their desired haven.

<sup></sup>³¹Let them give thanks unto the Lord for His mercy,
  And for His wonderful works to the children of men!
³²Let them exalt Him also in the assembly of the people,
  And praise Him in the seat of the elders.
³³He turneth rivers into a wilderness,
  And watersprings into a thirsty ground;
³⁴A fruitful land into a salt waste,
  For the wickedness of them that dwell therein.
³⁵He turneth a wilderness into a pool of water,
  And a dry land into watersprings.
³⁶And there He maketh the hungry to dwell,
  And they establish a city of habitation;
³⁷And sow fields, and plant vineyards,
  Which yield fruits of increase.
³⁸He blesseth them also, so that they are multiplied greatly,
  And suffereth not their cattle to decrease.
³⁹Again, they are minished and dwindle away
  Through oppression of evil and sorrow.
⁴⁰He poureth contempt upon princes,
  And causeth them to wander in the waste, where there
    is no way.
⁴¹Yet setteth He the needy on high from affliction,
  And maketh his families like a flock.
⁴²The upright see it, and are glad;
  And all iniquity stoppeth her mouth.
⁴³Whoso is wise, let him observe these things,
  And let them consider the mercies of the Lord.

The theme of Psalm 107 is sounded in the very first verse:

¹"O give thanks unto the Lord, for He is good,
  For His mercy endureth for ever."

We encountered this same refrain in Psalms 106, 118, and 136. Outside of Psalms we hear its echo in Ezra, chapter 3. Here it serves to establish the argument of this entire psalm. Psalm 107 is a joyous expression of appreciation of God's saving power, presenting four discrete vignettes that depict an instance of God's mercy. Significantly, each of the vignettes can be seen as describing God's help to individual people, or they can be interpreted as describing the experience of the entire Israelite people in the course of their exile to Babylonia and their return to their homeland. This latter interpretation is suggested most strongly by verses 2 and 3:

> ²So let those redeemed of the Lord say,
>   Whom He hath redeemed from the hand of the adversary;
> ³And gathered them out of the lands
>   From the east and from the west,
>   From the north and from the south.

In such a reading, verses 2–9 are about the people being sent into exile. Verses 10–16 can be read as describing their captivity. Verses 23–32 perhaps reflect the experiences of some of the former captives returning home over the sea. Verses 36–38 and 39–40 can be seen as describing more generally the process of return from exile.

Yet something is lost in this more collectivist reading. While other psalms are clearly about the shared experience of the entire nation, Psalm 107 reads more meaningfully as describing God's mercy to different classes of individuals. In this reading, verses 4–9 would describe anyone wandering through the wilderness, which we can choose to read literally, as referring more generally to people lost in an unfamiliar environment, or, in an altogether metaphorical fashion, as depicting people lost and adrift. Verses

10–16 would be about God's mercy to captives, and verses 23–32 would be about people who journey on the sea. It is verses 17–22 that have special relevance to us here, and have no place in a more national interpretation. These verses are clearly about people suffering from illness.

Again we note the connection between illness and transgression in verse 17, but just as we saw in previously examined psalms, we can find significance in what this psalm says about illness without accepting the idea that illness is a punishment for wrongdoing. In this psalm we encounter a more concrete depiction of illness with the reference to "rejection of food" in verse 18. But in the context of this psalm, the focus is not on the anguish of sickness, but on the assurance of God's mercy—and God's saving help.

The psalm assures us that God's mercy is extended to people in all four of these classes: the lost, the captive, the sea journeyer, and the person suffering from illness. Because these groups are only mentioned as examples, God's mercy extends to all people in all predicaments. God can save us because God controls people's circumstances (verses 33–38), both physical (verses 33–35) and political (verses 39–40). Above all, God protects those in need (verse 41).

The fundamental belief expressed in Psalm 107 is reinforced in the very last words of the psalm: "And let them consider the mercies of the Lord." It is also made explicit in the chorus that appears near the end of each of the vignettes: "Let them give thanks unto the Lord for His mercy / And for His wonderful works to the children of men!" (verses 8, 15, 21, and 31). It is articulated, as well, in the refrain that echoes throughout the psalm: "They cried unto the Lord in their trouble / And He brought them out of their distresses" (verses 6, 13, 19, and 28).

For people suffering from illness this general assurance might be comfort enough. But the psalm makes special note of people struggling with sickness and offers them special words of hope. That special promise is found in verse 20: "He sent His word, and healed them / And delivered them from their graves." Even if we find ourselves at the very brink of death, this verse assures us, God can deliver and heal us. When we are suffering from illness, the words that echo throughout the psalm, and the verses that begin and end it, can have special meaning, and hold out special hope.

This same theme of thanksgiving is found in Psalm 30.

²I will extol Thee, O Lord, for Thou hast raised me up,
  And hast not suffered mine enemies to rejoice over me.
³O Lord my God,
  I cried unto Thee, and Thou didst heal me;
⁴O Lord, Thou broughtest up my soul from the nether-world;
  Thou didst keep me alive, that I should not go down
    to the pit.
⁵Sing praise unto the Lord, O ye His godly ones,
  And give thanks to His holy name.
⁶For His anger is but for a moment,
  His favour is for a life-time;
  Weeping may tarry for the night,
  But joy cometh in the morning.
⁷Now I had said in my security:
  "I shall never be moved."
⁸Thou hadst established, O Lord, in Thy favour my mountain
    as a stronghold—
  Thou didst hide Thy face; I was affrighted.
⁹Unto Thee, O Lord, did I call,
  And unto the Lord I made supplication:
¹⁰"What profit is there in my blood, when I go down to
    the pit?

Shall the dust praise Thee? shall it declare Thy truth?
<sup>11</sup>Hear, O Lord, and be gracious unto me;
   Lord, be Thou my helper."
<sup>12</sup>Thou didst turn for me my mourning into dancing;
   Thou didst loose my sackcloth, and gird me with gladness;
<sup>13</sup>So that my glory may sing praise to Thee, and not be silent;
   O Lord my God, I will give thanks unto Thee for ever.

Once again we encounter the theme of enemies, and again we can read it figuratively as alluding to the author's adversities. In this psalm it seems most likely that the psalmist is, in fact, talking about an illness, and rejoicing at recovery from it (verse 3). We have explored (in chapter 4) the ways God's participation is enlisted in the psalmist's travail. Clearly the pleas of the author of Psalm 30 were heard. God preserved the psalmist's life, bringing the psalmist back from the very brink of death (verse 4). God, who is praised elsewhere as a healer, is here called "helper" (verse 11). The author's joy is jubilantly articulated in the closing two verses. Psalm 30 is a powerful affirmation of one who has faced illness and prevailed.

If Psalm 107 began to deal concretely with the reality of illness, Psalm 38 goes further still. The connection between illness and punishment is present here (verses 4, 5, 19) as it is elsewhere, but it is clearly incidental and the reference has the feel of having been included out of a sense of obligation. Allusions to enemies are also present (verses 13, 20, 21) and we can again choose to ignore them or interpret them allegorically. But the mention of enemies in Psalm 38 has an interesting twist. These enemies are depicted as vital and robust, in contrast to the psalmist's condition (verse 20). Psalm 38 is clearly about someone struggling with illness:

²O Lord, rebuke me not in Thine anger;
  Neither chasten me in Thy wrath.
³For Thine arrows are gone deep into me,
  And Thy hand is come down upon me.
⁴There is no soundness in my flesh because of thy
      indignation;
  Neither is there any health in my bones because of my sin.
⁵For my iniquities are gone over my head;
  As a heavy burden they are too heavy for me.
⁶My wounds are noisome, they fester,
  Because of my foolishness.
⁷I am bent and bowed down greatly;
  I go mourning all the day.
⁸For my loins are filled with burning;
  And there is no soundness in my flesh.
⁹I am benumbed and sore crushed;
  I groan by reason of the moaning of my heart.
¹⁰Lord, all my desire is before Thee;
  And my sighing is not hid from Thee.
¹¹My heart fluttereth, my strength faileth me;
  As for the light of mine eyes, it also is gone from me.
¹²My friends and my companions stand aloof from my plague;
  And my kinsmen stand afar off.
¹³They also that seek after my life lay snares for me;
  And they that seek my hurt speak crafty devices,
  And utter deceits all the day.
¹⁴But I am as a deaf man, I hear not;
  And I am as a dumb man that openeth not his mouth.
¹⁵Yea, I am become as a man that heareth not,
  And in whose mouth are no arguments.
¹⁶For in Thee, O Lord, do I hope;
  Thou wilt answer, O Lord my God.

17 For I said: "Lest they rejoice over me;
   When my foot slippeth, they magnify themselves
      against me."
18 For I am ready to halt,
   And my pain is continually before me.
19 For I do declare mine iniquity;
   I am full of care because of my sin.
20 But mine enemies are strong in health;
   And they that hate me wrongfully are multiplied.
21 They also that repay evil for good
   Are adversaries unto me, because I follow the thing
      that is good.
22 Forsake me not, O Lord;
   O my God, be not far from me.
23 Make haste to help me,
   O Lord, my salvation.

Psalm 38 is filled with descriptions of the author's illness. The psalmist's body is afflicted (verse 8) and the psalmist feels oppressed and the despondency that often accompanies physical illness (verse 9). There are references to pain and physical infirmity throughout the psalm—in verses 3, 4, 5, 6, 7, 8, 9, 11, 14, 15, and 18. In fact, we cannot read this psalm without having an almost physical response to the psalmist's pain and affliction.

The author feels abandoned by family and friends (verse 12) and affronted by the joy of adversaries at the weakness the psalmist is forced to endure. Unlike some of the psalms we have looked at, this is not a psalm of rejoicing or thanksgiving. It is a full-throated cry for help. This psalm does not give us the experience of a crisis addressed and resolved. Rather, it allows us to enter the inner spiritual world of someone in the midst of travail.

The author has not experienced healing. Instead the psalm gives us fellow-feeling for someone desperately ill and looking for help from God. Psalm 38 gives voice to what each of us feels in the midst of our own illness, or what we feel on behalf of dear ones as they struggle with theirs. Psalm 38 is a psalm we read when we feel ourselves overcome by our afflictions, calling out to God to be present with us and pleading for God's assistance. The psalmist's allusion to family and friends standing aloof (verse 12) serves a special purpose. If they keep themselves far from us, surely God can behave differently from them and draw close to help us (verses 22, 23).

This psalm offers us help in putting our own travail and concern into words. As we read it, it makes our plea for us. Jewish tradition teaches that every person who visits someone when they are ill takes one-seventieth of the illness away with them. This psalm, when we invite its company in our suffering, takes away at least that much.

A similar theme is found in Psalm 6, although it is developed with more literary sophistication and ultimately leads in a very different direction. In this psalm, no connection is made between illness and punishment for sin. The psalmist's sufferings are taken on their own terms. The theme of enemies is given only the most passing mention (verses 8, 11) and, as elsewhere, can easily be construed as referring to adversities. We can read this psalm as addressing all manner of travail, but it makes most sense if we understand it, like Psalm 38, as describing the agony of someone in the throes of serious illness.

> [1]O Lord, rebuke me not in Thine anger,
> Neither chasten me in Thy wrath.
> [3]Be gracious unto me, O Lord, for I languish away;
> Heal me, O Lord, for my bones are affrighted.

⁴My soul also is sore affrighted;
  And Thou, O Lord, how long?
⁵Return, O Lord, deliver my soul;
  Save me for Thy mercy's sake.
⁶For in death there is no remembrance of Thee;
  In the nether-world who will give Thee thanks?
⁷I am weary with my groaning;
  Every night make I my bed to swim;
  I melt away my couch with my tears.
⁸Mine eye is dimmed because of vexation;
  It waxeth old because of all mine adversaries.
⁹Depart from me, all ye workers of iniquity;
  For the Lord hath heard the voice of my weeping.
¹⁰The Lord hath heard my supplication;
  The Lord receiveth my prayer.
¹¹All mine enemies shall be ashamed and sore affrighted;
  They shall turn back, they shall be ashamed suddenly.

The pain and suffering of the protagonist are rendered graphically in this psalm. The author describes the feeling of languishing away, bones shot through with anxiety and pain (verse 3). We experience the author's groaning and crying. Even eyesight fails from sheer weariness (verse 8). In this inventory of afflictions, we can hear the all-too-familiar anguish of someone in the midst of grave illness. We may well recognize it from sitting by the beds of pain of loved ones, or from lying in our own.

One element of this psalm that makes it so effective is the pathetic quality of the description of the sufferer's agony. This vivid and realistic depiction of what it is to be ill evokes our empathy, and captures what we have experienced when we or our loved ones were in that very situation. As with Psalm 38, its cry of pain becomes our own, and its call for God to intervene expresses our innermost hopes.

But there is one significant way in which Psalm 6 differs dramatically from Psalm 38. As in Psalm 38, the psalmist seeks to involve God in the struggle against illness. Using the same rhetorical strategy as Psalm 30 (30:10), the psalmist argues that if death prevails, God will have no further benefit from the author's existence (verse 6). Unlike Psalm 38, Psalm 6 ends on a note of hope. At the conclusion, the psalmist rejoices that God has heard the supplication offered, "receiveth my prayer" (verse 10). The final note is one of triumph. The ending can give us confidence in our own encounters with illness that hope can prevail, that our calls for help will be heard. But it is not only the positive denouement that makes Psalm 6 so different from Psalm 38. There is yet one other element that constitutes the power of Psalm 6.

The most remarkable aspect of Psalm 6 is not the affirmation that God hears and saves, but the pervasive sense throughout the psalm of God's closeness. More than any other psalms we have examined in this chapter, this psalm resonates with a sense of profound intimacy with a God who is close at hand and is readily available to be called on in times of distress. Perhaps that is why it is included among the traditional penitential psalms that are part of the daily liturgy.

The interaction with God is very personal in Psalm 6. The psalmist models a relationship in which we can argue with, even chastise, God (verse 4). At one point the author calls on God to respond to us for God's own sake (verse 5). The notion of "for your own sake" is often hard for us to understand, but it will make sense if we recognize that it assumes a relationship so intimate and so intense that God's own well-being is, indeed, understood as being bound up with that of the petitioner—as is, in truth, the case among family, close friends, and lovers. A remarkable audacious idea perhaps, but one that is at the foundation of many of the human–divine relationships we encounter in the Bible, and certainly the one described here.

We can see still another aspect of the intimacy of this relationship in verse 6. We noted earlier that in this verse the psalmist's argument rests on the remarkable idea that God's own best interests are served by the author's recovery. If we regard it objectively, we could characterize such an assertion as manipulative, and it well may be. The truth is that such manipulation is, in fact, possible, but it can only take place in the context of a relationship where real intimacy exists. It would be inappropriate and unfeasible in a relationship that was anything but truly close. It is the intensity of the relationship depicted here that makes such an argument possible. The conditions exist for it to be, in fact, the case that God's own well-being would be diminished by the death of someone with whom God was indeed bound up. The theology of this psalm is not based on intellectual comprehension nor a theology of commandment. This psalm is founded on the theology of relationship.

We have seen this kind of relationship with God among the giants of the biblical saga. Abraham argued with God (Genesis 18:16–33). Moses did so repeatedly (as in Exodus 32:11–35). Psalm 6 assures us that ordinary people like ourselves can aspire to that quality of relationship as well. It gives us permission to remonstrate with God, and actively entreat God to intervene in our cause. Indeed, by the very act of reading the psalm, and making its words and intentions our own, we have entered into just such a relationship. The psalm opens the door for us to relate to God in a way that makes it possible for us to enlist God in our struggle. When we call upon God in the midst of our illness, it is not an imposition; it is what our relationship entitles us to. It is that permission for engagement, even more than the successful outcome of such an engagement here (verse 9), that gives this psalm its power and makes it especially precious in our times of need.

A story is told about one of the Chasidic rabbis. As he lay on his sickbed, his disciples gathered about him, anxious for his recovery. Suddenly his young grandson broke through the circle of disciples and rushed to his grandfather's bed. "So, do you have anything you would like to say to God?" the grandfather asked. The boy burst out, "Please God, make my grandfather well." The disciples burst into laughter at the audacity of such an impudent request. The *rebbe* stilled them by saying, "If you can't pray for what you really want, what good is prayer?"

That is the spirit of Psalm 6. It reminds all of us that if you can't pray for what you really want, what good is prayer?

## Participating in the Drama of Healing — with the Psalms

The cumulative effect of all the psalms we have looked at is to remind us of several lessons. They teach us that illness, no less than health, is part of what it is to be a human being. Each of us, and each of our dear ones, has times when illness becomes the dominant reality of our lives. These times cannot be dismissed as aberrations, and certainly should not be regarded as punishment for some wrongdoing. They are, rather, an integral part of the human experience.

These psalms remind us that we do not have all the resources within ourselves to help us through these times of trial. We have to look beyond ourselves to those who are entrusted with our care, to our friends and our family for support and nurture. The psalms tell us that there is help and healing that comes, as well, from beyond the earthly realm.

One important way the psalms help us is by teaching us to understand God as healer. This concept can be interpreted metaphorically: God makes whole the shattered, mends all the brokennesses in our lives. But it is an idea that can be taken more literally as well. God is healer of the sick. Calling on God as *rofeh* (healer) attests to our recognition of God as the ultimate source of all that contributes to our recovery. The psalms open to us the possibility of understanding that God is there for us to call upon for help and healing in our time of need.

As we read the psalms we become participants in the drama of petition and response, of illness and healing. Entering into the world of the psalms helps us make our way into a relationship with God in which we can enlist God as a helper and healer on our behalf in the face of our distress. At the beginning of this chapter, we encountered Moses interceding on behalf of his sister Miriam during her illness. Just as he cried out in his time of need, so the psalms allow us to call out in ours—and be answered: "O God, please God. . . . Heal us and we shall be healed."

# 6

*Fight Against Them That Fight Against Me*

# WHEN IT FEELS LIKE
# ENEMIES SURROUND US

O f all the figures in the Bible, none looms larger—or receives a more three-dimensional depiction—than Moses. We often think of the term lawgiver to describe him. We also recognize that he must have been an inspiring leader to take a group of runaway slaves and forge them into a cohesive and effective nation. Jewish tradition elevates one dimension of his personality by referring to him as *Rabbeinu* (our teacher), and understands him as the archetypal caring, patient instructor of those who would follow in his ways. *Midrash,* Jewish mythical elaboration on the biblical text, renders the young Moses as a "good shepherd" who would not rest until he had discovered and rescued a single lost sheep who had wandered away from the flock.

Other images of Moses are plentiful: the endangered infant we first encounter in a basket set afloat on the Nile; the hero who waded into potential danger to drive away a group of shepherds harassing the daughters of the Midianite priest Reuel (Exodus 2:16–20). But the image of Moses as a terrified fugitive fleeing for his life from pursuers? That is not one most of us would quickly call to mind. Yet that is how Moses is portrayed in a significant episode at the very beginning of his career:

> Some time after that, when Moses had grown up, he went out to his kinfolk and witnessed their toil. He saw an Egyptian beating a Hebrew, one of his kinsmen. He turned this way and that and, seeing no one about, he struck down the Egyptian and hid him in the sand. When he went out the next day, he found two Hebrews fighting; so he said to the offender, "Why do you strike your fellow?" He retorted, "Who made you chief and ruler over us? Do you mean to kill me as you killed the Egyptian?" Moses was frightened, and thought: Then the matter is known! When Pharaoh learned of the matter, he sought to kill Moses; but Moses fled from Pharaoh. He arrived in the land of Midian, and sat down beside a well.               (Exodus 2:11–15)

Moses in danger, running for his life, fearing the wrath of pursuers who wished to do him harm. This is an image of Moses seldom recollected, and yet pivotal in his career. Interestingly, it is not the only instance of a biblical figure in such jeopardy. The prophet Elijah also knew the wrath of people of power, and terror at their intentions toward him.

Elijah is one of the most compelling figures we meet in the later sections of the biblical canon. He was a man whose episodic career included roaming about the countryside providing help and care to the poorest and most in need, help that often involved the performance of miracles. More significantly, Elijah was both passionately devoted to God and unable to restrain himself from denouncing those whom he saw as deviating from God's ways either in their reversion to idol worship or in the way they treated other people. In one well-known incident, Elijah won the enmity of the powerful and vindictive Queen Jezebel by defeating and decimating the prophets of Baal, the Canaanite god whom she worshipped. As described in the Book of First Kings, Elijah understood his life to be in danger and fled her wrath:

> When Ahab told Jezebel all that Elijah had done and how he
> had put all the prophets to the sword, Jezebel sent a messenger to Elijah, saying, "Thus and more may the gods do if by
> this time tomorrow I have not made you like one of them."
>
> Frightened, he fled at once for his life. He came to
> Beer-sheba, which is in Judah, and left his servant there; he
> himself went a day's journey into the wilderness. He came
> to a broom bush and sat down under it, and prayed that he
> might die. "Enough!" he cried. "Now, O Lord, take my life,
> for I am no better than my fathers."      (1 Kings 19:1–4)

Can we begin to imagine how Moses felt about the Pharaoh whose minions were pursuing him, or how Elijah felt about the powerful Queen and the troops she deployed to destroy him? Their feelings were not very different, perhaps, from those of another biblical figure, David, who left a rich and diverse trove of images—shepherd-boy, defeater of Goliath, musician, warrior, lover, consolidator of disparate tribes, and founder of a dynasty.

David's life was full and variegated, but never calm. He appears to have been in frequent (one could almost say constant) jeopardy. Indeed through much of his story, he is in flight for his life: from his pathologically jealous predecessor on the throne, King Saul; from the Philistines; from his own rebellious son Absalom; and from the constant turmoil and intrigue within his palace. David is a man who knew danger and who recognized that he had enemies, which may be one reason the authorship of the Book of Psalms has traditionally been ascribed to him.

One aspect of the psalms that comes into focus as we study them is a pattern of references to—even preoccupation with—enemies. The psalms alludes to enemies who plot against, or pursue the protagonist, enemies who gloat over the author's misfortune. The world of the psalmist is one in which you know there are people who hate you, and people who you hate.

## Me? Have Enemies?

There is a part of us that is profoundly uncomfortable with such assertions. We would prefer to see our world as one in which enmity between people does not exist. Certainly we would rather view ourselves as people who do not have enemies. Perhaps we want to think of ourselves as incapable of inspiring hatred in others, or not being the kind of people who could feel animosity toward others.

While there are such people in the world, people with no enemies, they are precious few: the saintly, the pure-hearted. Jewish tradition refers to such people as *tzaddikim,* the righteous. One such *tzaddik* left a record of his reflections on the subject of hatred in his personal prayer, which has been preserved in the Jerusalem Talmud:

> May it be Your will O Lord my God and God of my fathers
> That no one's heart be taken over by hatred for me
> and that hatred for no person should take over my heart
> That jealousy of me should not take over the heart of
>   any person
> and that jealousy of any person should not take over
>   my heart . . .
>
> (J. Berachot 7d)

People like this can be found in the world and have always existed, but Jewish tradition suggests that there are only a mere handful of *tzaddikim* in every generation.

If we look at our own lives objectively, we most likely conclude that although *tzaddik*-hood is a noble goal for us to aspire to, we fall short of achieving it. That does not make us evil, only human. The Chasidic teacher Rabbi Schneur Zalman of Lyadi wrote that there are three classes of human beings. Some are *tzaddikim*—but not many. Some are altogether wicked and depraved. Mercifully there are very few of these. The vast majority of people he calls *benoni*—in between: neither altogether wicked nor altogether righteous. Almost all of us are *benoni*.

To be *benoni* means that there are times when we are capable of doing things that cause others to feel wrath, animosity, and even hatred toward us. And it means that there are times when we harbor these feelings toward others. To be honest with ourselves means to admit that there have been occasions when it has felt as if, merited or not, somebody has wanted to do us harm; someone has wished the worst for us.

To be *benoni* is to experience what Moses, Elijah, and David felt in their times of crisis. You do not have to be a giant like them to have enemies. The novelist Saul Bellow once noted "even paranoiacs have enemies." Well could we note, in this context, even average, ordinary, everyday people have enemies. How do we respond to the fact of someone else's animosity? What do we feel toward those people whom we see as our enemies? These are very uncomfortable questions for all of us who aspire to be better than we are, who have *tzaddik*-hood, or simple human decency, as our goal. Yet they are questions that all of us are forced to confront at various times, even while in the midst of striving to make ourselves better. The Book of Psalms is an important resource at those times when we feel there are enemies in our lives.

## Encounters with Enemies in the Psalms

Enemies seem to be almost omnipresent in psalms. They crop up in the most unexpected places. We have already encountered them in our discussion of sickness. Enemies are mentioned in Psalms 6:11; 30:2; 38:13, 17, 20–21; and 41:3 and 6–12. In that context the phrase could have signified adversities just as easily as human adversaries. But the plain meaning of these texts does suggest enemies who gloated over the author's misfortunes.

The theme of enemies taking pleasure in the protagonist's distress is one that is sounded elsewhere in Psalms. We find it in Psalm 13:

> ³How long shall I take counsel in my soul,
> Having sorrow in my heart by day?
> How long shall mine enemy be exalted over me?
> ⁴Behold Thou, and answer me, O Lord my God;
> Lighten mine eyes, lest I sleep the sleep of death;
> ⁵Lest mine enemy say: "I have prevailed against him";
> Lest mine adversaries rejoice when I am moved.
> (Psalm 13:3–5)

We find in Psalms, as well, a sense of not just one but a *host* of enemies arrayed against the psalmist. This is captured in a powerful image in Psalm 69.

> ⁵They that hate me without cause are more numerous
>     than the hairs on my head.
> They that would cut me off, being my enemies wrongfully,
>     are many . . .
> (Psalm 69:5)

Ideally, none of us would ever have such sentiments. But realistically, haven't there been times when this is how it felt in your life? The sense of frustration and desperation that we encounter here is articulated even more movingly in Psalm 89:

39But Thou hast cast off and rejected,
  Thou hast been wroth with Thine anointed.
40Thou hast abhorred the covenant of Thy servant;
  Thou hast profaned his crown even to the ground.
41Thou hast broken down all his fences;
  Thou hast brought his strongholds to ruin.
42All that pass by the way spoil him;
  He is become a taunt to his neighbours.
43Thou hast exalted the right hand of his adversaries;
  Thou hast made all his enemies to rejoice.
44Yea, Thou turnest back the edge of his sword,
  And hast not made him to stand in the battle.
45Thou hast made his brightness to cease,
  And cast his throne down to the ground.
46The days of his youth hast Thou shortened;
  Thou hast covered him with shame.
  (Psalm 89:39–46)

It is not difficult to see how Jewish tradition might identify this psalm as being "of David." References to God's anointed (verse 39), a throne cast to the ground (verse 40), and defeat in battle (verse 44) recall events in David's life. Yet viewed not as history but as metaphor, these verses offer a glimpse into the inner world of any person who has felt defeated in some painful situation in life—and vanquished by adversaries.

Psalms such as these not only put our own feelings into words, but also give us the comfort of recognizing ourselves in

someone else's situation. The psalms tell us that everybody has
times like these, times when we feel impotent in the face of people we perceive as working against us, times when we feel rage at
those we see as laboring for our defeat.

The lurking presence of those enemies erupts in even the
most serene and pastoral of the psalms. In the midst of the green
pastures and still waters of Psalm 23, there are fleeting allusions to
those who would do us harm: "Thou preparest a table before me
in the presence of mine enemies . . ." (Psalm 23:5). Those adversaries, seen only sketchily in Psalm 23, are seen more vividly in
Psalm 7:

> ²O Lord my God, in Thee have I taken refuge;
>   Save me from all them that pursue me, and deliver me;
> ³Lest he tear my soul like a lion,
>   Rending it in pieces, while there is none to deliver.
> ⁴O Lord my God, if I have done this;
>   If there be iniquity in my hands;
> ⁵If I have requited him that did evil unto me,
>   Or spoiled mine adversary unto emptiness;
> ⁶Let the enemy pursue my soul, and overtake it,
>   And tread my life down to the earth;
>   Yea, let him lay my glory in the dust.
>   (Psalm 7:2–6)

Enemies are described even more violently and ferociously
elsewhere:

> ³Why boastest thou thyself of evil, O mighty man?
>   The mercy of God endureth continually.
> ⁴Thy tongue deviseth destruction;
>   Like a sharp razor, working deceitfully.

5 Thou lovest evil more than good;
Falsehood rather than speaking righteousness.
6 Thou lovest all devouring words,
The deceitful tongue.
(Psalm 52:3–6)

5 My soul is among lions, I do lie down among them that
are aflame;
Even the sons of men, whose teeth are spears and arrows,
And their tongue a sharp sword.
(Psalm 57:5)

12 He is like a lion that is eager to tear in pieces,
And like a young lion lurking in secret places.
(Psalm 17:12)

19 Thou hast let loose thy mouth for evil,
And thy tongue frameth deceit.
20 Thou sittest and speakest against thy brother;
Thou slanderest thine own mother's son.
(Psalm 50:19–20)

Although these enemies truly personify ferocious ill will, in reality they may not have been as violent or terrifying as they are depicted. (Of course, if the protagonist was, in fact, King David, then his military opponents may have been as violent and blood-thirsty as described here.) The adversaries we encounter in our lives are most likely not as ferocious as those depicted by the psalmist. But when we find ourselves in the midst of conflict—whatever its nature—our adversaries do appear like this to us.

My suspicion is that verses such as these act as a Rorschach test: Each reader automatically supplies his or her own identification of the destructive predators described in the text. We tend to view these verses not as allusions to historical figures who lived thousands of years ago, or as vague literary references, but as very real and potent inhabitants of our everyday lives.

There is solace in finding our personal nemeses in the pages of this ancient text. Psalms reminds us, once again, that we are not alone in the most painful situations of our lives. In our darkest moments we may feel especially cursed or singled out for unusual suffering. Psalms tells us that others have been there before and that, through the ages, countless others have turned to Psalms for comfort precisely because they, too, have gone through what we are now experiencing.

## Taking a Closer Look at Our Human Reflex to Revenge

Having in our world a person, or group of people, whom we feel to be hostile toward us or to our best interests, is, it seems—like sickness—an inescapable part of what it is to be human. All of us would rather avoid these experiences, and perhaps a blessed few of us do. But the vast majority of us must walk the tortuous path through the valley of this affliction, too.

It is not an easy path out. It is tempting to get mired in our fear or rage. As part of discovering that we do have enemies, it seems most natural to wish to fight them and triumph over them. There is much in Psalms about vengeance and retribution. To read such verses when things are tranquil in our lives is disturbing, almost painful. When we read them in the midst of crisis, they make a different kind of sense, as the psalmist gives full voice to the rage we feel when we perceive ourselves to be in jeopardy:

> 24 My tongue also shall tell of Thy righteousness all the day;
>   For they are ashamed, for they are abashed, that seek
>     my hurt . . .
> (Psalm 71:24)

¹⁰Oh that a full measure of evil might come upon the wicked,
  And that Thou wouldest establish the righteous;
  For the righteous God trieth the hearts and reins.
  (Psalm 7:10)

This attitude, which can be fairly characterized by the term "vengeful," erupts elsewhere in Psalms in various contexts. Indeed, the desire to see those the psalmist identifies as evildoers punished animates an entire psalm:

³Why boastest thou thyself of evil, O mighty man?
  The mercy of God endureth continually.
⁴Thy tongue deviseth destruction;
  Like a sharp razor, working deceitfully.
⁵Thou lovest evil more than good;
  Falsehood rather than speaking righteousness.
⁶Thou lovest all devouring words,
  The deceitful tongue.
⁷God will likewise break thee for ever,
  He will take thee up, and pluck thee out of thy tent,
  And root thee out of the land of the living.
⁸The righteous also shall see, and fear,
  And shall laugh at him:
⁹"Lo, this is the man that made not God his stronghold;
  But trusted in the abundance of his riches,
  And strengthened himself in his wickedness."
¹⁰But as for me, I am like a leafy olive-tree in the house of God;
  I trust in the mercy of God for ever and ever.
¹¹I will give Thee thanks for ever, because Thou hast done it;
  And I will wait for Thy name, for it is good, in the presence
    of Thy saints.
  (Psalm 52:3–11)

The sentiments articulated in these psalms model a stance reiterated in the liturgy that was based on the Book of Psalms. In the twelfth benediction of the *Amidah*—the central prayer of Judaism's daily service—we read:

> For slanderers, let there be no hope. Let all wickedness perish as in a moment. Let all Your enemies be quickly cut off. May You uproot and shatter, cast down and humble the dominion of arrogance quickly and in our time. Blessed are You, O Lord, who shatters the enemy and humbles the arrogant.

We cannot read these words without being reminded of their antecedents in Psalms.

The theme of retribution serves as the concluding note in a disconcertingly large number of psalms. Of these, Psalm 1:6 is representative: "For the Lord regardeth the way of the righteous; / But the way of the wicked shall perish." The same attitude is given voice at the conclusion of numerous other psalms:

> [20]The Lord preserveth all them that love Him;
> But all the wicked will He destroy.
> (Psalm 145:20)

> [11]All the horns of the wicked also will I cut off;
> But the horns of the righteous shall be lifted up.
> (Psalm 75:11)

> [9]Keep me from the snare which they have laid for me,
> And from the gins of the workers of iniquity.
> [10]Let the wicked fall into their own nets,
> Whilst I withal escape.
> (Psalm 141:9–10)

¹¹For Thy name's sake, O Lord, quicken me;
    In Thy righteousness bring my soul out of trouble.
¹²And in Thy mercy cut off mine enemies,
    And destroy all them that harass my soul;
    For I am Thy servant.
    (Psalm 143:11–12)

¹¹The righteous shall rejoice when he seeth the vengeance;
    He shall wash his feet in the blood of the wicked.
¹²And men shall say: "Verily there is a reward for the
        righteous;
    Verily there is a God that judgeth in the earth."
    (Psalm 58:11–12)

The most distressing in this genre of endings is that of Psalm 137, an otherwise lovely and moving psalm. Psalm 137 begins with, "By the rivers of Babylon, / there we sat down, / yea, we wept / when we remembered Zion." It also contains the stirring assertion:

⁵If I forget thee, O Jerusalem,
    Let my right hand forget her cunning.
⁶Let my tongue cleave to the roof of my mouth,
    If I remember thee not;
    If I set not Jerusalem
    Above my chiefest joy.
    (Psalm 137:5–6)

But then comes the chillingly violent imprecation against the nation responsible for the exile of the Jews:

⁷Remember, O Lord, against the children of Edom
    The day of Jerusalem;

Who said: "Rase it, rase it,
Even to the foundation thereof."
⁸O daughter of Babylon, that art to be destroyed;
Happy shall he be, that repayeth thee
As thou hast served us.
⁹Happy shall he be, that taketh and dasheth thy little ones
Against the rock.
(Psalm 137:7–9)

Not the noblest of emotions, but our own; they reflect what most of us feel in the midst of travail. Even if we are not proud of such sentiments, we can identify them as being profoundly human.

What sense can we make of these *benoni* feelings? They may be akin to the darker emotions we experience in the midst of mourning. None of us who has lost a loved one would welcome having to experience that pain again. Most people would just as soon deny feelings of loss and pain, lock them up in a closet, and walk away from them. But traditional Jewish practice makes it virtually impossible for us to do that.

The Jewish rites of mourning force us to recognize our grief and anguish during the *shiva,* the seven days following the funeral. They announce to the world—and to us—that we are not quite ourselves during the *shloshim,* the thirty days after the death of a loved one. Indeed, during the entire first year after a death, Jewish practices have the effect of reminding survivors that they are not yet ready to re-enter the normal pattern of life. Instead, they are impelled to acknowledge that they are broken, not altogether whole.

The same psychological perspective, I believe, that lies behind Jewish mourning practices, shapes the use people have made of the psalms' treatment of rage at "the enemy." Much as we would like to deny such feelings within ourselves, we are driven to acknowledge their existence.[1]

As with mourning, the only way to get past these "darker" feelings is to go through them. We cannot get them out of our systems until we acknowledge they were in our systems in the first place. In mourning, only by allowing ourselves to descend into the depths of falling apart can we hope to put ourselves back together. In rage, only by acknowledging our emotions can we avoid giving them dominion over us. Once we have owned the feelings we would rather not have, we can begin to take the actions necessary to put them behind us. Finding our own sentiments mirrored in the words of Psalms serves as an opportunity to immerse ourselves in those feelings as a necessary step toward putting ourselves on the path to getting beyond them.

## *Recognizing Our Need for Help*

Beyond the desire for revenge and retribution we experience during times of assault is our recognition of our overwhelming need for help. Even as we look for human allies to come to our aid, we come to understand our need for God's assistance. References in psalms to the desire for victory over adversaries and for revenge are frequent, but even more numerous are the pleas to God to rally to the psalmist's salvation.

The cry for help is woven through many of the psalms. The words may be ancient, but the feelings they articulate are immediate and compelling to us when we feel ourselves under assault.

> [3]I will cry unto God Most High;
> Unto God that accomplisheth it for me.
> [4]He will send from heaven, and save me,
> When he that would swallow me up taunteth.
> (Psalm 57:3–4)

²O my God, in Thee have I trusted, let me not be ashamed;
Let not mine enemies triumph over me.
(Psalm 25:2)

¹⁹Consider how many are mine enemies,
And the cruel hatred wherewith they hate me.
²⁰O keep my soul, and deliver me;
Let me not be ashamed, for I have taken refuge in Thee.
(Psalm 25:19–20)

¹⁶My times are in Thy hand;
Deliver me from the hand of mine enemies, and from
them that persecute me.
(Psalm 31:16)

³How long shall I take counsel in my soul,
Having sorrow in my heart by day?
How long shall mine enemy be exalted over me?
⁴Behold Thou, and answer me, O Lord my God;
Lighten mine eyes, lest I sleep the sleep of death;
⁵Lest mine enemy say: "I have prevailed against him";
Lest mine adversaries rejoice when I am moved.
(Psalm 13:3–5)

⁸Keep me as the apple of Thy eye,
Hide me in the shadow of Thy wings,
⁹From the wicked that oppress,
My deadly enemies, that compass me about.
(Psalm 17:8–9)

*There are people out there who would do me harm and I need Your help.* Often we do not have the words to make this urgent request.

The above, as elsewhere, express our needs better than we can, often in beautiful language and with compelling imagery.

In several instances, the cry for God's help becomes the basis for an entire composition. In these cases the plea is extended, employing the elements we have already noted: recognition of the existence of the enemy, a desire for revenge against the enemy, and a call for God's assistance and salvation. Such an extended cry for help is Psalm 59:

> [2] Deliver me from mine enemies, O my God;
> Set me on high from them that rise up against me.
> [3] Deliver me from the workers of iniquity,
> And save me from the men of blood.
> [4] For, lo, they lie in wait for my soul;
> The impudent gather themselves together against me;
> Not for my transgression, nor for my sin, O Lord.
> [5] Without my fault, they run and prepare themselves;
> Awake Thou to help me, and behold.
> [6] Thou therefore, O Lord God of hosts, the God of Israel,
> Arouse Thyself to punish all the nations;
> Show no mercy to any iniquitous traitors.
> [7] They return at evening, they howl like a dog,
> And go round about the city.
> [8] Behold, they belch out with their mouth;
> Swords are in their lips;
> "For who doth hear?"
> [9] But Thou, O Lord, shalt laugh at them;
> Thou shalt have all the nations in derision.
> [10] Because of his strength, I will wait for Thee;
> For God is my high tower.
> [11] The God of my mercy will come to meet me;
> God will let me gaze upon mine adversaries.

¹²Slay them not, lest my people forget,
   Make them wander to and fro by Thy power, and bring
      them down,
   O Lord our shield.
¹³For the sin of their mouth, and the words of their lips,
   Let them even be taken in their pride,
   And for cursing and lying which they speak.
¹⁴Consume them in wrath, consume them, that they be
      no more;
   And let them know that God ruleth in Jacob,
   Unto the ends of the earth.
¹⁵And they return at evening, they howl like a dog,
   And go round about the city;
¹⁶They wander up and down to devour,
   And tarry all night if they have not their fill.
¹⁷But as for me, I will sing of Thy strength;
   Yea, I will sing aloud of Thy mercy in the morning;
   For Thou has been my high tower,
   And a refuge in the day of my distress.
¹⁸O my strength, unto Thee will I sing praises;
   For God is my high tower, the God of my mercy.

Psalm 59 is a wonderful literary work, with its stark and powerful images and consistently evocative language. The psalm is tightly and intricately constructed. Certain words, phrases, and images are repeated, creating an integrated whole. The phrase "all the nations" is repeated in verses 6 and 9, three different verbs for singing are employed in verses 17 and 18. The image in verse 7 is repeated and elaborated in verses 15–16. And various parts of the day are mentioned throughout the composition: the day as a whole in verse 17; morning in verse 17; evening in verses 7 and 15; and night in verse 16.

Some of the words that are repeated convey themes central to the meaning of the psalm. Thus God's strength is invoked in verses 10, 17, and 18. The image of God as *misgav* (high tower) is found in verses 10, 17, and 18, and the root word from which this noun is derived is employed as a verb in verse 2 ("Set me on high"). God is enjoined to "awake" in verse 5 and "arouse Thyself" in verse 6. The words "deliver me" or "save me" are found at the beginning of both verse 2 and verse 3. The carefully repeating construction of Psalm 59 contributes to the power we feel in it as we read it.

Part of Psalm 59 reads as if its subject was the fate of the entire nation. The images of the enemy encircling the city in verses 6 and 15 suggest a military conflict. The use of the phrase "all the nations" in verses 6 and 9 can, similarly, suggest a nationalist reading of the psalm. But nothing else in the psalm gives that same collectivist sense. Moreover, the sense of the rest of the psalm and its first-person singular construction (see "save me from the men of blood," verse 3) suggest that this psalm is the outcry of a single individual beset by enemies. (It is entirely possible that the more nationalistic verses were added at a later period, perhaps in the midst of a national crisis.) Certainly most readers of the psalm will identify with the protagonist calling for God's help in the face of "them that rise up against me" (verse 2).

We meet those enemies at the very beginning of the psalm. Their description in verse 8 is ferocious, and reminiscent of Psalms 57:5, 52:4, and 64:4. We see them plotting against the psalmist and devising their plans (verses 4, 5). The psalmist calls upon God "Awake Thou to help me . . ." (verse 5). Presumptuous as these words may appear to us, they are similar to the accusatory sentiments we find throughout the Book of Psalms, often in even starker terms:

> [12]Thou has given us like sheep to be eaten;
> And hast scattered us among the nations.
> (Psalm 44:12)

We find similar language in Psalms 3:8, 7:7, 9:20, 10:12, 17:13, 35:2, 35:23, 44:27, 68:2, 74:22, and 82:8. An image very much like this is in this psalm in verse 6.

In passing, as we talk about rousing God from slumber, it is of interest to note that elsewhere in Psalms a contrasting assertion is made:

> [2]My help cometh from the Lord,
> Who made heaven and earth.
> [3]He will not suffer thy foot to be moved;
> He that keepeth thee will not slumber.
> [4]Behold, He that keepeth Israel
> Doth neither slumber nor sleep.
> (Psalm 121:2–4)

## God: Just Like Us? Examining the Problem of Images

Certainly these images have heavily anthropomorphic overtones—they describe God as resembling human beings. But so do many of the images in Psalms, and throughout the Bible for that matter. Yet we do not have to understand such images in literal terms to be moved by them. We do not have to believe that God has literally been asleep to appreciate the sense in which God is being called to summon all the divine potencies and marshal them on our behalf.

More significantly, language such as this may seem presumptuous to us. That very presumption may be what makes Psalm 59 so powerful. It reflects a relationship with God that can only be characterized as intimate. The psalmist enjoys a closeness with God that becomes ours as the psalmist's words become our own. By giving expression to the intensity of that relationship, the psalmist opens a door for us to find our way to such intimacy of our own.

The psalmist cries out, as might be expected, to be saved in verses 2 and 3. More troubling, but as elsewhere in Psalms, the psalmist also calls for retribution. The author calls on God to "punish all the nations" (verse 6). More violent and graphic forms of retribution are described in verses 12 and 14. We have already noted in Psalms the reflexive desire for retribution against our enemies.

In the midst of the desire for retribution, we come upon a most unexpected image. The psalmist envisions God as laughing at the enemies (verse 9). Whatever anthropomorphic images we might be familiar with, we are hardly accustomed to thinking of God laughing. Yet the image of God laughing at our enemies is a crucial part of the retribution the psalmist wishes against those enemies. This captivating image is used in a similar way in other psalms:

> 4 He that sitteth in heaven laugheth,
> The Lord hath them in derision.
> (Psalm 2:4)

> 13 The Lord doth laugh at him;
> For He seeth that his day is coming.
> (Psalm 37:13)

This image captures in a compelling way the sense of what it is to have God as our ally. Most likely it is more comfortable for us to think of God laughing in derision at our enemies than killing them.

The last verses of Psalm 59 give it a changed meaning. We hear jubilation in these final verses:

> ¹⁷But as for me, I will sing of Thy strength;
>   Yea, I will sing aloud of Thy mercy in the morning;
>   For Thou has been my high tower,
>   And a refuge in the day of my distress.
> ¹⁸O my strength, unto Thee will I sing praises;
>   For God is my high tower, the God of my mercy.

In passing, we should take note of the image of *misgav* (high tower), which we noted earlier. It stands in contrast to the many anthropomorphic images of God that cause some modern readers a degree of discomfort. The Book of Psalms is rich in metaphors like this, which describe and help us think of God in images drawn from outside the realm of human experience. When we are troubled by the psalms'—and other parts of the Bible's—recourse to anthropomorphisms, images like this remind us that such metaphors are just a few among many ways of representing a God who, in the end, is beyond all of the images we use. As a *misgav*, God is a tangible place of salvation for us. The high tower may serve as the promontory from which we can gain strategic advantage over our enemies. Or perhaps it can serve as a refuge in which we can be raised above the fray.

Verses 17 and 18 have a different sense than the verses that precede them. They sound as if the salvation that the psalmist cried out for in the rest of the psalm has occurred—as if a reversal of fortune took place between verses 16 and 17. Now, rather than beseeching God to be a high tower, the psalmist praises God for being precisely that. By the end of Psalm 59, God has changed from being a God we cry out for to a God who saves. This is a profound transition, one that has powerful implications for us in our own times of need. In light of its closing verses, Psalm 59 becomes a drama of desperation and salvation.

Many of the same elements noted in Psalm 59 can be found in Psalm 35, with one significant addition:

¹Strive, O Lord, with them that strive with me;
  Fight against them that fight against me.
²Take hold of shield and buckler,
  And rise up to my help.
³Draw out also the spear, and the battle-axe, against them
    that pursue me;
  Say unto my soul: "I am thy salvation."
⁴Let them be ashamed and brought to confusion that seek
    after my soul;
  Let them be turned back and be abashed that devise
    my hurt.
⁵Let them be as chaff before the wind,
  The angel of the Lord thrusting them.
⁶Let their way be dark and slippery,
  The angel of the Lord pursuing them.
⁷For without cause have they hid for me the pit,
    even their net,
  Without cause have they digged for my soul.
⁸Let destruction come upon him unawares;
  And let his net that he hath hid catch himself;
  With destruction let him fall therein.
⁹And my soul shall be joyful in the Lord;
  It shall rejoice in His salvation.
¹⁰All my bones shall say: "Lord, who is like unto Thee,
  Who deliverest the poor from him that is too strong
    for him,
  Yea, the poor and the needy from him that spoileth him?"

¹¹ Unrighteous witnesses rise up;
  They ask me of things that I know not.
¹² They repay me evil for good;
  Bereavement is come to my soul.
¹³ But as for me, when they were sick, my clothing was
    sackcloth
  I afflicted my soul with fasting;
  And my prayer, may it return into mine own bosom.
¹⁴ I went about as though it had been my friend or my
    brother;
  I bowed down mournful, as one that mourneth for
    his mother.
¹⁵ But when I halt they rejoice, and gather themselves
    together;
  The abjects gather themselves together against me,
    and those whom I know not;
  They tear me, and cease not;
¹⁶ With the profanest mockeries of backbiting
  They gnash at me with their teeth.
¹⁷ Lord, how long wilt Thou look on?
  Rescue my soul from their destructions,
  Mine only one from the lions.
¹⁸ I will give Thee thanks in the great congregation;
  I will praise thee among a numerous people.
¹⁹ Let not them that are wrongfully mine enemies rejoice
    over me;
  Neither let them wink with the eye that hate me without
    a cause.
²⁰ For they speak not peace;
  But they devise deceitful matters against them that are
    quiet in the land.

21 Yea, they open their mouth wide against me;
   They say: "Aha, aha, our eye hath seen it."
22 Thou hast seen, O Lord; keep not silence;
   O Lord, be not far from me.
23 Rouse Thee, and awake to my judgment,
   Even unto my cause, my God and my Lord.
24 Judge me, O Lord my God, according to Thy righteousness;
   And let them not rejoice over me.
25 Let them not say in their heart: "Aha, we have our desire;"
   Let them not say: "We have swallowed him up."
26 Let them be ashamed and abashed together that rejoice
      at my hurt;
   Let them be clothed with shame and confusion that
      magnify themselves against me.
27 Let them shout for joy, and be glad, that delight in my
      righteousness;
   Yea, let them say continually: "Magnified be the Lord,
   Who delighteth in the peace of His servant."
28 And my tongue shall speak of Thy righteousness,
   And of Thy praise all the day.

The images of Psalm 35 are vivid. The description of the enemies' wickedness is stark:

15 They tear me and cease not;
16 With the profanest mockeries of backbiting
   They gnash at me with their teeth.

The call for the defeat and punishment of the enemies makes use of violent and martial images. God is depicted as a warrior in full regalia (verses 2, 3). As in Psalm 59, the psalmist calls on God to rise up (verses 2, 23). Distasteful as such militaristic imagery might be to modern sensibilities, it is not without precedent elsewhere in the Bible.

> The Lord is my strength and might; He is become my salvation. This is my God and I will enshrine Him; The God of my father, and I will exalt Him. The Lord, the Warrior—Lord is His name!                    (Exodus 15:2–3)

> See, then, that I, I am He; There is no god beside Me. I deal death and give life; I wounded and I will heal: None can deliver from My hand. Lo, I raise My hand to heaven and say: As I live forever, When I meet My flashing blade and My hand lays hold on judgment, vengeance will I wreak on My foes, will I deal to those who reject Me. I will make drunk My arrows with blood—as My sword devours flesh—blood of the slain and the captive from the long-haired enemy chiefs.
>
> O nations, acclaim His people! For He'll avenge the blood of His servants, wreak vengeance on His foes, and cleanse the land of His people.   (Deuteronomy 32:39–43)

This is imagery that appealed to people in a more militaristic period of time, but it does not speak to the life experiences of most of us, and has thus lost its power to move us on a literal level. Still it exists as a powerful metaphor for a God who rises to our aid, a forceful ally in time of desperate need.

The call for God's assistance in Psalm 35 is vividly articulated in verse 1: "Strive, O Lord, with them that strive with me; / Fight against them that fight against me." This verse clearly served as the model for the seventh benediction of the *Amidah,* included in the daily liturgy, which states:

Look upon our affliction, fight our battles, and save us quickly for the sake of Your name. For You are a mighty savior. Blessed are You, O Lord, who saves Israel.

The psalmist goes to great lengths to underscore the fact that the enemies are filled with hate for no cause. This theme was also sounded in passing in Psalm 59, verse 4, "Not for my transgression, nor for my sin. . . ." Here that theme is elaborated. Verse 7 is devoted to that idea: "For without cause have they hid for me the pit, even their net, / Without cause have they digged for my soul." This theme is restated in verse 19. We encounter this same notion elsewhere in Psalms:

> 5 They that hate me without a cause are more than the hairs
>   of my head;
> They that would cut me off, being mine enemies wrongfully,
>   are many;
> Should I restore that which I took not away?
> (Psalm 69:5)

> 3 They compassed me about also with words of hatred,
> And fought against me without a cause.
> (Psalm 109:3)

In verses 12–14 of Psalm 35, the psalmist pleads that while the author acted benevolently toward them, these enemies "repay me evil for good." This idea is similar to the one put powerfully in Psalm 109, verses 4–5:

> 4 In return for my love they are my adversaries;
> But I am all prayer.
> 5 And they have laid upon me evil for good,
> And hatred for my love . . .

The psalmist's pain—and ours when we are in the psalmist's position—is increased by the sense that our enemies' hatred has no rational motivation. It is not based on anything that we have done to them. We feel hurt to have our love repaid with hatred. The psalmist beautifully captures our own psychological dynamic when we feel beset and cannot identify the reason.

## Reversal of Fortune to Our Own Advantage — Our Enemies' Disadvantage

In verse 8 of Psalm 35 we come upon an element that we have not encountered before. In other verses of this psalm, as in other psalms we have examined, the psalmist calls for retribution. In verse 8 the protagonist cries out:

> 8Let destruction come upon him unawares;
> And let his net that he hath hid catch himself;
> With destruction let him fall therein.

Not only does the psalmist want the enemy's plans thwarted and the enemy punished; here the psalmist calls for a particular kind of reversal of fortune—*may their own plans rebound against them. Let them be destroyed by the very instruments they had fashioned to use against me.* This plea for what we can call poetic justice is encountered in others of the psalms:

> 16He hath digged a pit, and hollowed it,
> And is fallen into the ditch which he made.
> 17His mischief shall return upon his own head,
> And his violence shall come down upon his own pate.
> (Psalm 7:16–17)

⁷They have prepared a net for my steps,
My soul is bowed down;
They have digged a pit before me,
They are fallen into the midst thereof themselves.
(Psalm 57:7)

It is also given explicit articulation in Psalm 28:4—

⁴Give them according to their deeds, and according to the
    evil of their endeavours;
Give them after the work of their hands;
Render to them their desert.

This attitude may seem familiar to those who have read the *Megillah* of Esther, which concludes with the villain Haman being hanged on the gallows he had prepared for the murder of the righteous Mordechai and all of the Jews:

> Now in the twelfth month, which is the month Adar, on the thirteenth day of the same, when the King's commandment and his decree drew near to be put in execution, in the day that the enemies of the Jews hoped to have rule over them; whereas it turned to the contrary, that the Jews had rule over them that hated them.          (Esther 9:1)

> . . . Haman . . . the enemy of all the Jews had devised against the Jews to destroy them; but when . . . [Esther] came before the King, he commanded by letters that his wicked device should return upon his own head; and that he and his sons should be hanged on the gallows . . .
> 
> (Esther 9:24–25)

The desire to have our enemies hoisted on their own petard has a special resonance when we feel ourselves to be the objects of other people's malicious designs.

The themes we have seen in the psalms we have examined are found, as well, in Psalm 64.

> ²Hear my voice, O God, in my complaint;
>   Preserve my life from the terror of the enemy.
> ³Hide me from the council of evil-doers;
>   From the tumult of the workers of iniquity;
> ⁴Who have whet their tongue like a sword,
>   And have aimed their arrow, a poisoned word;
> ⁵That they may shoot in secret places at the blameless;
>   Suddenly do they shoot at him, and fear not.
> ⁶They encourage one another in an evil matter;
>   They converse of laying snares secretly;
>   They ask, who would see them.
> ⁷They search out iniquities, they have accomplished a
>       diligent search;
>   Even in the inward thought of every one, and the deep
>       heart.
> ⁸But God doth shoot at them with an arrow suddenly;
>   Thence are their wounds.
> ⁹So they make their own tongue a stumbling unto
>       themselves;
>   All that see them shake the head.
> ¹⁰And all men fear;
>   And they declare the work of God,
>   And understand His doing.
> ¹¹The righteous shall be glad in the Lord, and shall take
>       refuge in Him;
>   And all the upright in heart shall glory.

The psalmist's plea is articulated straightforwardly at the out-set (verses 2–3). The description of the enemies sounds familiar to us from our experience with other psalms. Verse 4 is similar to 52:4, 55:22, 57:5, and 59:8, and highlights how many descriptions of the enemy in Psalms focus on violence located in the mouth. In our own experience, the truth is that we are more often wounded by peoples' words than by physical violence.

What is most striking about Psalm 64 is the dramatic shift between verses 7 and 8. While the first seven verses are a cry for help using themes and images we have encountered before, the final four verses are a description of God in the process of respond-ing. God, in verses 8–9, comes to the psalmist's defense and aid. In carefully constructed counterpoint to the earlier verses, verse 8—

> 8But God doth shoot at them with an arrow suddenly;
> Thence are their wounds.

—responds to the threat described in verse 5—

> 5That they may shoot in secret places at the blameless;
> Suddenly do they shoot at him, and fear not.

—and verse 9—

> 9So they make their own tongue a stumbling unto
>   themselves;
> All that see them shake the head.

—borrows the imagery of verse 4 to depict God saving the psalmist from the designs of the enemy. By depicting God in the act of saving the protagonist, Psalm 64 allows us to participate in the drama of salvation. The psalm ends with an evocation of words of praise and thanksgiving from onlookers who acknowledge, and rejoice in, God's saving power.

## Rejoicing in Being Rescued

Psalm 64 begins like a psalm that calls on God to help and save us, and concludes like a psalm of praise that gives thanks for being saved.

When we are in the midst of being threatened by enemies, it is hard to imagine that we can be saved from their designs on us. Psalm 64 *moves* us into a sense that salvation can, in fact, come for us. Many other psalms allow us to experience what it is to be rescued from peril and to rejoice in our salvation, including the theme of salvation in Psalm 3:

> 7I am not afraid of ten thousands of people,
>   That have set themselves against me round about.
> 8Arise, O Lord; save me, O my God;
>   For Thou hast smitten all mine enemies upon the cheek,
>   Thou hast broken the teeth of the wicked.
> 9Salvation belongeth unto the Lord;
>   Thy blessing be upon Thy people.
>   (Psalm 3:7–9)

The theme of rejoicing in being rescued resounds in Psalm 18:

> 4Praised, I cry, is the Lord,
>   And I am saved from my enemies.

³¹ As for God, His way is perfect;
The word of the Lord is tried;
He is a shield unto all them that take refuge in Him.
³² For who is God, save the Lord:
and who is a Rock, except our God?
³³ The God that girdeth me with strength,
And maketh my way straight;
³⁴ Who maketh my feet like hinds',
And setteth me upon my high places;
³⁵ Who traineth my hands for war,
So that mine arms do bend a bow of brass.
³⁶ Thou hast also given me Thy shield of salvation,
And Thy right hand hath holden me up;
And Thy condescension hath made me great.
³⁷ Thou has enlarged my steps under me,
And my feet have not slipped.
³⁸ I have pursued mine enemies, and overtaken them;
Neither did I turn back till they were consumed.
³⁹ I have smitten them through, so that they are not
able to rise;
They are fallen under my feet.
⁴⁰ For Thou hast girded me with strength unto the battle;
Thou hast subdued under me those that rose up
against me.
⁴¹ Thou hast also made mine enemies turn their backs unto me,
And I did cut off them that hate me.
⁴² They cried, but there was none to save;
Even unto the Lord, but He answered them not.
⁴³ Then did I beat them small as the dust before the wind;
I did cast them out as the mire of the streets.

<sup>49</sup>He delivereth me from mine enemies;
    Yea, Thou liftest me up above them that rise up against me;
    Thou deliverest me from the violent man.
    (Psalm 18:4, 31–43, 49)

The rhythm and imagery of these verses embody an energy
and vitality that mirrors the revitalizing content of their message.
As we read these words, the author's joy gives us hope that these
sentiments can become our own, along with the experience of
being rescued from the vicious designs of our enemies.

The exultant words of rejoicing from selected verses of various other psalms can be woven into a unified song:

<sup>1</sup>The Lord is my light and my salvation; whom shall I fear?
    The Lord is the stronghold of my life; of whom shall I
        be afraid?
<sup>2</sup>When evil-doers came upon me to eat up my flesh,
    Even mine adversaries and my foes, they stumbled and fell.
<sup>3</sup>Though a host should encamp against me,
    My heart shall not fear;
    Though war should rise up against me,
    Even then will I be confident.
<sup>4</sup>One thing have I asked of the Lord, that will I seek after:
    That I may dwell in the house of the Lord all the days
        of my life,
    To behold the graciousness of the Lord, and to visit
        early in His temple.
<sup>5</sup>For He concealeth me in His pavilion in the day of evil;
    He hideth me in the covert of His tent;
    He lifteth me up upon a rock.

⁶And now shall my head be lifted up above mine enemies
    round about me;
 And I will offer in His tabernacle sacrifices with
    trumpet-sound;
 I will sing, yea, I will sing praises unto the Lord.
 (Psalm 27:1–6)

⁸I will be glad and rejoice in Thy lovingkindness;
 For Thou has seen mine affliction,
 Thou hast taken cognizance of the troubles of my soul,
⁹And Thou hast not given me over into the hand of the
    enemy;
 Thou hast set my feet in a broad place.
 (Psalm 31:8–9)

⁶For though the Lord be high, yet regardeth He the lowly,
 And the haughty He knoweth from afar.
⁷Though I walk in the midst of trouble, Thou quickenest me;
 Thou stretchest forth Thy hand against the wrath of
    mine enemies,
 And Thy right hand doth save me.
 (Psalm 138:6–7)

⁶Behold, God is my helper;
 The Lord is for me as the upholder of my soul.
⁷He will requite the evil unto them that lie in wait for me;
 Destroy Thou them in Thy truth.
 (Psalm 54:6–7)

As we read these verses, the spirit of thanksgiving that characterizes them holds out hope and promise. We, too, can cry out

and be answered. Those who wish the worst for us can see their designs frustrated. We can find ourselves rescued from our peril, survive, and flourish.

Psalms assures us: The pit and the snare need not prevail. Those who create them may appear stronger than we are. But there is a Power greater even than theirs, a Power that can triumph over them. When we invite God to take our part, we can look forward to singing songs not only of petition, but ultimately of deliverance—and then of thanksgiving and praise. All of us long to have the assurance we hear in the words Moses used to address the Jewish people as they stood on the shore of the Red Sea:

> Have no fear! Stand by and witness the deliverance which
> the Lord will work for you today.          (Exodus 14:13)

The hope of the psalmist in the face of adversaries was given succinct articulation by another biblical poet, the prophet Isaiah. Isaiah's distillation of this spirit, which animates the psalms, can become an assurance in which we find confidence for ourselves:

> You may take counsel together—
> and it will come to nought,
> speak words about us
> and it will not avail
> For God is with us.
> (Isaiah 8:10)

We live in a world filled with adversities, peopled with adversaries. Psalms gives us courage to live in such a world. We find this first in the recognition that we are not alone in that situation; others have experienced it before us. Second, reading Psalms gives us confidence that the One who stood with the psalmists and thwarted the designs of their enemies can stand with us. In giving us the knowledge that God can be rallied to our defense, and affording us the means to rouse God to our cause, Psalms becomes the great treasure it is in our times of dire need.

# 7

*For Your Kindness Endures For Ever*

# GIVING THANKS

Your life is hanging by a thread, literally. At any second the thread could snap. It does not. Perhaps you know what it is to come to the very precipice, and to back away from it—you or someone dear to you: to be in a terrible automobile accident and walk away unscathed; to be stricken with a fatal illness and recover; to endure the most crushing reverses and be able to marshal your energies and rebuild your life. You have been granted a reprieve, a new start. How do you begin?

We live through that very experience in the biblical account of Esther. The King's Prime Minister, Haman, took deep personal offense at the refusal of Mordechai, the Jew, to bow down to him. In retaliation, Haman persuaded the King to issue an edict calling for the destruction of all Jews under his sovereignty. Mordechai appealed to his cousin, Queen Esther: Only she could intercede on behalf of her people. Perhaps, he added, she had risen to royal estate for just such a time as this.

Esther was overcome with fear. She knew that it was against the protocol of the palace for anyone to come into the King's presence without being specifically invited. In speaking with her,

Mordechai cast Esther's dilemma in stark relief. If she violated the protocol of the palace she could well be put to death. If she obeyed the protocol of the palace and did not intercede on behalf of her people, she would most likely perish along with them. Two paths opened before her—both leading to mortal jeopardy.

Esther anguished over which course to take. Finally she committed herself to action. She chose to approach the King. If he did not hold out his golden scepter to her, she would be doomed. She prepared for the worst. She asked her people to hold vigil for her. She would do what must be done; and, she added, "If I perish, I perish." (Esther 4:16) She entered the chamber of the King to plead her cause and, miraculously, he extended his golden scepter.

Narratively, the rest of the tale flows from this moment. Humanly, imagine what Esther must have felt when the King reached out to her, and her peril was averted.

## Using the Psalms to Put Our Thankfulness into Words

All of us have had times when things could have gone terribly wrong for us, and they did not. Emotionally, our first response is an overwhelming sense of gratitude. At times like this we experience the closeness of God, and search for ways to put our feelings of thankfulness into words.

As we have explored the Book of Psalms, we have seen the range of human conditions it evokes: illness; fear of abandonment; threat to our well-being. We have heard psalms give voice to the experiences of our lives and articulate our hopes. And we have seen how often the psalms depict the reversal of fortune we long for when our lives become difficult: illness supplanted by health; the overturning of the designs of those who would be our enemies; distance from God giving way to a sense of nearness. In so many of the psalms we have examined, the final act of the drama is restoration of wholeness and the expression of gratitude for this reversal of fortune.

In truth, the psalms are not only about hope. Often, they are about the fulfillment of hope. A significant portion of many of the psalms—and the entirety of others—is devoted to the expression of gratitude for the restoration of our well-being, and the goodness that characterizes our lives when they are going well. Not the least of the manifold gifts given to us by the Book of Psalms is its help in putting the gratitude we so often feel into words.

When our lives feel good to us, or have been restored to goodness after a crisis, we can feel ourselves in the words of Psalm 16:

> 5O Lord, the portion of mine inheritance and of my cup,
> Thou maintainest my lot.
> 6The lines are fallen unto me in pleasant places;
> Yea, I have a goodly heritage.
> 7I will bless the Lord, who hath given me counsel;
> Yea, in the night seasons my reins instruct me.
> 8I have set the Lord always before me;
> Surely He is at my right hand, I shall not be moved.
> 9Therefore my heart is glad, and my glory rejoiceth;
> My flesh also dwelleth in safety;
> 10For Thou wilt not abandon my soul to the nether-world;
> Neither wilt Thou suffer Thy godly one to see the pit.
> 11Thou makest me to know the path of life;
> In Thy presence is fulness of joy,
> In Thy right hand bliss for evermore.
> (Psalm 16:5–11)

These are the words of a person who is feeling wholly at one with God. Verse 8, which begins *"Shiviti Adonai L'negdi tamid"* (I have set the Lord always before me) has come to serve in Jewish tradition as the basis of the practice of putting a *"shiviti"* plaque in the home as a visible testimony to the absolute certainty of God's presence. The psalmist expresses not only gratitude, but complete confidence.

We encounter these very sentiments in the psalm that is probably the most familiar to us, Psalm 23:

> ¹The Lord is my shepherd; I shall not want.
> ²He maketh me to lie down in green pastures;
> He leadeth me beside the still waters.
> ³He restoreth my soul.
> He guideth me in straight paths for His name's sake.
> ⁴Yea, though I walk through the valley of the shadow
> of death,
> I will fear no evil,
> For Thou art with me;
> Thy rod and Thy staff, they comfort me.
> ⁵Thou preparest a table before me in the presence of
> mine enemies;
> Thou hast anointed my head with oil; my cup runneth over.
> ⁶Surely goodness and mercy shall follow me all the days
> of my life;
> And I shall dwell in the house of the Lord for ever.

Psalm 23 compels us with the beauty of its pastoral imagery. The idea of ourselves as sheep taken care of by God, the attentive shepherd, and the lushness of the green pasture and the tranquility of the still waters convey to us the sense of absolute security and well-being that is the theme of this psalm. The knowledge that God is with us even in the face of adversity—in the presence of enemies; in the very face of death—is the foundation upon which the psalmist's certainty rests. It is this sense of confidence that has made this psalm so beloved to centuries of readers, and so central to their personal faith.

Psalm 23 and Psalm 16 share an image of God directing our course, protecting us, and providing for our needs. In both psalms, the authors express an unshakable certainty in God, and the bedrock knowledge that God will take care of them. It is appropriate that both of these psalms conclude on the note of confidence that we will abide in God's presence forever. It is worthy of mention that numerous other psalms similarly convey this same sense of certitude by concluding on the theme of "for ever": Psalms 15, 18, 28, 30, 41, 48, 115, 117, and 121.

## *"My God in Whom I Trust"*: Betach *(Trust) as Part of Our Lives*

The theme of security and trust resonates throughout the Book of Psalms. We hear these sentiments spoken by someone whose life is tranquil, or by someone who has gone through life's storms and emerged secure on the other side. A few psalms, of many, will represent this group:

>² O clap your hands, all ye peoples;
>  Shout unto God with the voice of triumph.
>³ For the Lord is most high, awful;
>  A great King over all the earth.
>⁴ He subdueth peoples under us,
>  And nations under our feet.
>⁵ He chooseth our inheritance for us,
>  The pride of Jacob whom He loveth.
>⁶ God is gone up amidst shouting,
>  The Lord amidst the sound of the horn.

7 Sing praises to God, sing praises;
  Sing praises unto our King, sing praises.
8 For God is the King of all the earth;
  Sing ye praises in a skillful song.
9 God reigneth over the nations;
  God sitteth upon His holy throne.
10 The princes of the peoples are gathered together,
  The people of the God of Abraham;
  For unto God belong the shields of the earth;
  He is greatly exalted.
  (Psalm 47)


1 O thou that dwellest in the covert of the Most High,
  And abidest in the shadow of the Almighty;
2 I will say of the Lord, who is my refuge and my fortress,
  My God, in whom I trust,
3 That He will deliver thee from the snare of the fowler,
  And from the noisome pestilence.
4 He will cover thee with His pinions,
  And under His wings shalt thou take refuge;
  His truth is a shield and a buckler.
5 Thou shalt not be afraid of the terror by night,
  Nor of the arrow that flieth by day;
6 Of the pestilence that walketh in darkness,
  Nor of the destruction that wasteth at noonday.
7 A thousand may fall at thy side,
  And ten thousand at thy right hand;
  It shall not come nigh thee.
8 Only with thine eyes shalt thou behold,
  And see the recompense of the wicked.
9 For thou hast made the Lord who is my refuge,
  Even the Most High, thy habitation.

¹⁰There shall no evil befall thee,
Neither shall any plague come nigh thy tent.
¹¹For He will give His angels charge over thee,
To keep thee in all thy ways.
¹²They shall bear thee upon their hands,
Lest thou dash thy foot against a stone.
¹³Thou shalt tread upon the lion and asp;
The young lion and the serpent shalt thou trample
under feet.
¹⁴"Because he hath set his love upon Me, therefore will I
deliver him;
I will set him on high, because he hath known My name.
¹⁵He shall call upon Me, and I will answer him;
I will be with him in trouble;
I will rescue him, and bring him to honour.
¹⁶With long life will I satisfy him,
And make him to behold My salvation."
(Psalm 91)

Both of these psalms give voice to confident assurance of God's protection. Verses 11–12 of Psalm 91 convey a lovely image of God protecting the psalmist—and us. This image has caused this psalm to be characterized by many as "a Psalm of Protection." Certainly it is worthy of being recited when we feel a need to be protected.

In Psalm 91:2 we come upon the word *betach* (trust), the sense of absolute confidence in God. This word, which sounds one of the most important themes in the Book of Psalms, appears in some variant over fifty times in the 150 Psalms. From a few representative verses we can create a litany:

⁷For I trust not in my bow,
Neither can my sword save me.

[8]But Thou hast saved us from our adversaries,
  And hast put them to shame that hate us.
  (Psalm 44:7–8)

[8]Some trust[1] in chariots, and some in horses;
  But we will make mention of the name of the Lord our God.
  (Psalm 20:8)

[3]Put not your trust in princes,
  Nor in the son of man, in whom there is no help.
  (Psalm 146:3)

[8]It is better to take refuge in the Lord
  Than to trust in man.
[9]It is better to take refuge in the Lord
  Than to trust in princes.
  (Psalm 118:8–9)

[12]In God do I trust, I will not be afraid;
  What can man do unto me?
  (Psalm 56:12)

Psalm 47 evokes numerous images of monarchy to exalt God
(verse 9 employs the imagery of enthronement). It has a great
deal in common with Psalms 93 and 95–100, which are frequently called the "enthronement cycle" because they appear to depict
the actual enthronement or coronation of God. In all of them, the
psalmist depicts God's ascension to power, and God's rule over all
the earth. Other rulers are but flesh and blood; God's rule is forever. Other rulers have limited power; God is omnipotent. If all of
these psalms are not overtly about thanksgiving, they are manifest
expressions of absolute confidence in God's power and of awe at

God's glory. They are the words of one who celebrates God, has confidence in God's goodness, and certainty that God rules the world with attention to our needs, and in justice. In such vision is implicit thanksgiving.

A powerful image of confidence in God is employed in Psalm 125:

> [1] . . . They that trust in the Lord
> Are as mount Zion, which cannot be moved, but abideth
>     for ever.
> [2] As the mountains are round about Jerusalem,
> So the Lord is round about His people,
> From this time forth and for ever.
> (Psalm 125:1–2)

Here we find an imaginative use of geographical imagery. The city of Jerusalem becomes a symbol of God's protecting concern. We encounter again the use of the word *betach* (trust) and the concept of "for ever." The author of Psalm 125 has unshakable faith in God's protection.

## Ki Tov *(For God Is Good): Celebrating God in Our Lives*

This same theme has been sounded in many of the psalms we have examined in earlier chapters. It is the idea we have encountered at the heart of Psalms 103, 111, and 121.

The confidence at the core of these psalms is the beginning of praise. Explicit praise and exaltation are given full-throated voice in a great number of the psalms. Psalm 34 provides a powerful example:

> [2] I will bless the Lord at all times;
> His praise shall continually be in my mouth.

<sup>3</sup>My soul shall hear thereof, and be glad.
<sup>4</sup>O magnify the Lord with me,
  And let us exalt His name together.
<sup>5</sup>I sought the Lord, and He answered me,
  And delivered me from all my fears.
<sup>6</sup>They looked unto Him, and were radiant;
  And their faces shall never be abashed.
<sup>7</sup>This poor man cried, and the Lord Heard,
  And saved him out of all his troubles.
<sup>8</sup>The angel of the Lord encampeth round about them that
    fear Him,
  And delivereth them.
<sup>9</sup>O taste and see that the Lord is good;
  Happy is the man that taketh refuge in Him.
<sup>10</sup>O fear the Lord, ye His holy ones;
  For there is no want to them that fear Him.
<sup>11</sup>The young lions do lack, and suffer hunger;
  But they that seek the Lord want not any good thing.
<sup>12</sup>Come, ye children, hearken unto me;
  I will teach you the fear of the Lord . . .

<sup>16</sup>The eyes of the Lord are toward the righteous,
  And His ears are open unto their cry.
<sup>17</sup>The face of the Lord is against them that do evil,
  To cut off the remembrance of them from the earth.
<sup>18</sup>They cried, and the Lord heard,
  And delivered them out of all their troubles.
<sup>19</sup>The Lord is nigh unto them that are of a broken heart,
  And saveth such as are of a contrite spirit.
<sup>20</sup>Many are the ills of the righteous,
  But the Lord delivereth him out of them all.
<sup>21</sup>He keepeth all his bones;
  Not one of them is broken.

²²Evil shall kill the wicked;
  And they that hate the righteous shall be held guilty.
²³The Lord redeemeth the soul of His servants;
  And none of them that take refuge in Him shall be desolate.
  (Psalm 34:1–12, 16–23)

Psalm 34 is another acrostic, each verse beginning with a successive letter of the Hebrew alphabet. The verses express praise for protection and deliverance. The effect of the whole is jubilant celebration of God's redemptive powers. There is no way to read this psalm without hearing in it a "back-story" of some crisis from which the psalmist was saved. That makes this psalm all the more meaningful for us when circumstances become our own, when our own life situation reflects that of the psalmist.

Of the individual verses of the psalm, regular participants in Jewish worship services may recognize verse 4, "O magnify the Lord with me, / And let us exalt His name together," which has been included in the traditional Torah service. Similarly, verse 23, "The Lord redeemeth the soul of His servants; / And none of them that take refuge in Him shall be desolate," is often included in the liturgy of Jewish funeral services.

Verse 16 uses graphic anthropomorphisms to turn depictions of physical attributes ascribed to God into powerful images of God's attentive concern for the righteous. God's "eyes" look out for their well-being, and God's ears are attuned to their needs. This verse is followed by one invoking God's "face" as being turned against those who do evil. The psalm's use of anthropomorphic imagery conveys ideas that could not be expressed as powerfully in less concrete form.

Verse 9 is intriguing, too, in the way it makes use of the human senses. It enjoins us, "O taste and see that the Lord is good *(ki tov)*". This mixing of senses can be understood as the result of an encounter with God so euphoric that the ecstatic one "sees" with the eyes that which has been "tasted" with the mouth. It is the testimony of one who has been overcome by a sense of thankfulness. In that regard, it is representative of the entire psalm—a powerful expression of gratitude.

The phrase *ki tov*—"that [the Lord] is good"—which appears in verse 9, has an interesting history. It is the same phrase we encounter in the first chapter of Genesis, where God at the end of each day of creation looks at the handiwork of that day and sees *ki tov*—that it was good. A little later in Genesis, the same phrase is associated with the first act of human disobedience: When Eve looked at the fruit of the tree she had been forbidden to eat and saw that in appearance it was good *(ki tov)* to eat (Genesis 3:6). From that perception, flowed the actions that would leave their imprint on the condition of human life for all generations to follow.

I like the connection between Genesis 3:6 and Psalm 34:9. In both places it is something we do with our mouth that causes us to "see" that it "is good." In Genesis, Adam and Eve taste the fruit and then "see that it was good." In Psalm 34 we "taste and see" that it is good. We could imagine that the act of praising God in this psalm is intended as atonement for the act of disobedience in the Genesis story.

In the Book of Psalms, wherever we find the phrase *"ki tov,"* it betokens an expression of praise and gratitude:

> ¹O give thanks to the Lord, for God is good [ki tov],
> God's mercy endures forever.
> (Psalms 106:1; 107:1; 118:1, 29; 136:1)

> ¹Hallelujah;
> For it is good [ki tov] to sing praises unto our God;

For it is pleasant, and praise is comely.
(Psalm 147:1)

8 With a freewill-offering will I sacrifice unto Thee;
 I will give thanks unto Thy name, O Lord, for it is good
   [ki tov].
(Psalm 54:8)

Similar use of *ki tov* in conjunction with praise of God is found in Psalms 52:11, 63:4, 69:17, and 109:21.

The celebration of God's saving power is found in the first half of Psalm 40. Although the second half of this psalm is, in reversal of what we might expect, a plea for God's intercession, the first verses make exultant celebration of God's redemption and are the ones of interest to us here. These verses put into words what any of us can feel when we have been saved from disaster.

2 I waited patiently for the Lord;
 And He inclined unto me, and heard my cry.
3 He brought me up also out of the tumultuous pit,
   out of the miry clay;
 And He set my feet upon a rock, He established my goings.
4 And He hath put a new song in my mouth, even praise
   unto our God;
 Many shall see, and fear,
 And shall trust in the Lord.
5 Happy is the man that hath made the Lord his trust,
 And hath not turned unto the arrogant, nor unto such
   as fall away treacherously.
6 Many things hast Thou done, O Lord my God,
 Even Thy wondrous works, and Thy thoughts toward us;

There is none to be compared unto Thee!
If I would declare and speak of them,
They are more than can be told.
(Psalm 40:2–6)

Here we have the evocation of absolute confidence in God
that we noted in earlier psalms. The word *betach* (trust) is repeated in verses 4 and 5. But this psalm goes further to celebrate overtly the fact that God has performed acts of salvation. The psalmist
moves beyond trust and confidence toward thanksgiving.

## Giving Thanks to God: Exploring Psalms of Praise

In each of the earlier chapters, we have seen verses in which the
psalmist sang songs of thanks when peril of one type or another
gave way to salvation. We will now look at a few instances, selected
from many, in which thanksgiving is the major theme of the
psalm.

Many psalms speak in tones of thanksgiving for God's assistance to the nation as a whole. We have examined expressions of
national thanksgiving before. We look at a few more here:

²O God, we have heard with our ears, our fathers have
   told us;
 A work Thou didst in their days, in the days of old.
³Thou with Thy hand didst drive out the nations, and didst
   plant them in;
 Thou didst break the peoples, and didst spread them
   abroad.
⁴For not by their own sword did they get the land in
   possession,
 Neither did their own arm save them;

But Thy right hand, and Thine arm, and the light of
    Thy countenance,
  Because Thou wast favourable unto them.
5Thou art my King, O God;
  Command the salvation of Jacob.
6Through Thee do we push down our adversaries;
  Through Thy name do we tread them under that rise
    up against us.
7For I trust not in my bow,
  Neither can my sword save me.
8But Thou hast saved us from our adversaries,
  And hast put them to shame that hate us.
9In God have we gloried all the day,
  And we will give thanks unto Thy name for ever.
  (Psalm 44:2–9)


1. . . . When the Lord brought back those that returned to Zion,
  We were like unto them that dream.
2Then was our mouth filled with laughter,
  And our tongue with singing;
  Then said they among the nations:
  "The Lord hath done great things with these."
3The Lord hath done great things with us;
  We are rejoiced.
4Turn our captivity, O Lord,
  As the streams in the dry land.
5They that sow in tears
  Shall reap in joy.
6Though he goeth on his way weeping that beareth
    the measure of seed,
  He shall come home with joy bearing his sheaves.
  (Psalm 126)

In these verses, and other psalms—9, 46, 47, 48, 66, 124, and 148—the psalmist expresses gratitude for God having saved the people as a whole. We can just as easily read these psalms as giving voice to our own personal rejoicing, and use them to give thanks for the help we feel we have received in our times of need. Along with the psalmist, we can feel radical amazement at the good that has been done for us, as expressed so powerfully in Psalm 126:1. There are times when our lot is so good that we feel, indeed, like those who dream. The songs of national thanksgiving can well be our own.

Yet many of the psalms speak in unabashedly individual and personal terms, expressing thanks for the author's good fortune. As we read these outpourings of personal gratitude, the words can articulate not only the psalmist's delight, but also our own. Each of us has experienced times when we were moved to exult just as the psalmist does:

¹Hallelujah,
  Praise the Lord, O my soul.
²I will praise the Lord while I live;
  I will sing praises unto my God while I have my being.
  (Psalm 146:1–2)

³³I will sing unto the Lord as long as I live.
  (Psalm 104:33)

⁷Sing unto the Lord with thanksgiving,
  Sing praises upon the harp unto our God . . .
  (Psalm 147:7)

⁸My heart is steadfast, O God, my heart is steadfast;
  I will sing, yea, I will sing praises.

9Awake, my glory; awake, psaltery and harp;
  I will awake the dawn.
10I will give thanks unto Thee, O Lord, among the peoples;
  I will sing praises unto Thee among the nations.
11For Thy mercy is great unto the heavens,
  And Thy truth unto the skies.
  (Psalm 57:8–11)[2]

The musician singer is moved to song, in gratitude to God. We share the exaltation and thanksgiving that these words articulate and evoke.

These same emotions—and some of the same imagery—are expressed in Psalm 92:

1A Psalm, A Song. For the Sabbath day.
2It is a good thing to give thanks unto the Lord,
  And to sing praises unto Thy name, O Most High;
3To declare Thy lovingkindness in the morning,
  And Thy faithfulness in the night seasons,
4With an instrument of ten strings, and with the psaltery;
  With a solemn sound upon the harp.
5For Thou, Lord, hast made me glad through Thy work;
  I will exult in the works of Thy hands.
6How great are Thy works, O Lord!
  Thy thoughts are very deep.
7A brutish man knoweth not,
  Neither doth a fool understand this.
8When the wicked spring up as the grass,
  And when all the workers of iniquity do flourish;
  It is that they may be destroyed for ever.
9But Thou, O Lord, art on high for evermore.
10For, lo, Thine enemies, O Lord,

For, lo, Thine enemies shall perish;
All the workers of iniquity shall be scattered.
11 But my horn hast Thou exalted like the horn of the wild-ox;
I am anointed with rich oil.
12 Mine eye also hath gazed on them that lie in wait for me,
Mine ears have heard my desire of the evil-doers that
rise up against me.
13 The righteous shall flourish like the palm-tree;
He shall grow like a cedar in Lebanon.
14 Planted in the house of the Lord,
They shall flourish in the courts of our God.
15 They shall still bring forth fruit in old age;
They shall be full of sap and richness;
16 To declare that the Lord is upright,
My Rock, in whom there is no unrighteousness.

In Psalm 92, more specific information about the conditions of the psalm's composition is added to the outpouring of thanksgiving. We sense that the psalmist is expressing gratitude for some actual occurrence of redemption. Though this psalm is self-identified as "for the Sabbath" (and as a result has been included in the traditional Sabbath liturgy), we are left with the impression that the author celebrates a particular event in which the "workers of iniquity" (verse 10) were defeated and the psalmist, in righteousness, prevailed. Here the tone of personal thanksgiving is explicit and the joy of salvation palpable. In reading these words we enter into the psalmist's delight; we may also use this distillation of that redemption to give expression to our own celebration and gratitude.

If the experience behind Psalm 92 is reconstructed through conjecture, the one behind Psalm 116 is depicted for us explicitly:

¹I love that the Lord should hear
 My voice and my supplications.
²Because He hath inclined His ear unto me,
 Therefore will I call upon Him all my days.
³The cords of death compassed me,
 And the straits of the nether-world got hold upon me;
 I found trouble and sorrow.
⁴But I called upon the name of the Lord:
 "I beseech Thee, O Lord, deliver my soul."
⁵Gracious is the Lord, and righteous;
 Yea, our God is compassionate.
⁶The Lord preserveth the simple;
 I was brought low, and He saved me.
⁷Return, O my soul, unto thy rest;
 For the Lord hath dealt bountifully with thee.
⁸For Thou has delivered my soul from death,
 Mine eyes from tears,
 And my feet from stumbling.
⁹I shall walk before the Lord
 In the lands of the living.

This exultant composition is clearly the work of one who has faced mortal peril and was spared. The psalmist calls out to God—as we so often do when confronted with crisis—and God hears (verses 1–2). That same image (borrowing, as it does from the human experience) has resonance in biblical tradition. The simple words "and God heard" in Exodus 2:24 represent the beginning of the process of liberation and redemption of the Hebrew slaves. They constitute the ball-bearing upon which all the rest of the events of the Exodus turn. God "hearing" is an image we encounter with some frequency in Psalms, in 6:9–10, 10:17, 17:1, 28:1–2, 28:6, 54:4, 55:3, 55:18, 55:20, 61:1, 61:6, 64:2 and 65:3.

God hearing our cry marks the onset of our reversal of fortune. That hearing, and all that devolves from it, are what the psalmist, and we who share the psalmist's experience, celebrate in these words. We look into the face of certain destruction, whatever its nature, and we are saved. Psalm 116 helps us to give thanks.

That same sense of God being attentive to us and reversing certain peril that lay in store for us is expressed in the central verses of Psalm 138:

> [1] I will give Thee thanks with my whole heart,
>   In the presence of the mighty will I sing praises unto Thee.
> [2] I will bow down toward Thy holy temple,
>   And give thanks unto Thy name for Thy mercy and for
>     Thy truth;
>   For Thou hast magnified Thy word above all Thy name.
> [3] In the day that I called, Thou didst answer me;
>   Thou didst encourage me in my soul with strength.
>
> [6] For though the Lord be high, yet regardeth He the lowly,
>   And the haughty he knoweth from afar.
> [7] Though I walk in the midst of trouble, Thou quickenest me;
>   Thou stretchest forth Thy hand against the wrath of
>     mine enemies,
>   And Thy right hand doth save me.
>   (Psalm 138:1–3, 6–7)

Rudiments of a story that may well be our own are set out. We experience jeopardy (verse 7). We call out (verse 3). God hears us, attends to us (verse 6), reverses the course of our fate, and saves us (verse 7). At the end of the experience we can only do what the psalmist has done: give thanks (verses 1–2). As we read the words of Psalm 116, the psalmist's experience and ours merge, and words of thanksgiving become our own.

## *Drawing on the Psalms' Power in Bad Times and Good Times Alike*

In earlier chapters we looked at the various kinds of trials that are an inescapable part of every human life. All of us would just as soon avoid them; none of us can. We have other moments in our lives, moments of triumph over our adversities, salvation from our perils; times when we feel accomplishment and joy, contentment and fulfillment. Just as it is right for us to cry out for God's help during times of distress, we can also look for words to express our thanks when fortune turns in our favor. And just as the Book of Psalms can be a resource when we cry out for help, it can also assist us in putting our gratitude into words. We have already looked at numbers of psalms that express confidence and trust, and others that give thanks. None put thanksgiving into words more jubilantly than Psalm 145:

> ¹I will extol Thee, my God, O King;
>   And I will bless Thy name for ever and ever.
> ²Every day will I bless Thee;
>   And I will praise Thy name for ever and ever.
> ³Great is the Lord, and highly to be praised;
>   And His greatness is unsearchable.
> ⁴One generation shall laud Thy works to another,
>   And shall declare Thy mighty acts.
> ⁵The glorious splendour of Thy majesty,
>   And Thy wondrous works, will I rehearse.
> ⁶And men shall speak of the might of Thy tremendous acts;
>   And I will tell of Thy greatness.

<sup>7</sup> They shall utter the fame of Thy great goodness,
  And shall sing of Thy righteousness.
<sup>8</sup> The Lord is gracious, and full of compassion;
  Slow to anger, and of great mercy.
<sup>9</sup> The Lord is good to all;
  And His tender mercies are over all His works.
<sup>10</sup> All Thy works shall praise Thee, O Lord;
  And Thy saints shall bless Thee.
<sup>11</sup> They shall speak of the glory of Thy kingdom,
  And talk of Thy might;
<sup>12</sup> To make known to the sons of men His mighty acts,
  And the glory of the majesty of His kingdom.
<sup>13</sup> Thy kingdom is a kingdom for all ages,
  And Thy dominion endureth throughout all generations.
<sup>14</sup> The Lord upholdeth all that fall,
  And raiseth up all those that are bowed down.
<sup>15</sup> The eyes of all wait for Thee,
  And Thou givest them their food in due season.
<sup>16</sup> Thou openest Thy hand,
  And satisfiest every living thing with favour.
<sup>17</sup> The Lord is righteous in all His ways,
  And gracious in all His works.
<sup>18</sup> The Lord is nigh unto all them that call upon Him,
  To all that call upon Him in truth.
<sup>19</sup> He will fulfill the desire of them that fear Him;
  He also will hear their cry, and will save them.
<sup>20</sup> The Lord preserveth all them that love Him;
  But all the wicked will He destroy.
<sup>21</sup> My mouth shall speak the praise of the Lord;
  And let all flesh bless His holy name for ever and ever.

Joy and exultation radiate from this psalm, and an ecstatic sense of gratitude touches and moves us. The words give powerful expression to the thanks we feel when things are going well for us.

Psalm 145 is another of those acrostics we encounter in the Book of Psalms—like Psalms 25, 34, 111, and 119—in which each verse begins with a successive letter of the alphabet. This acrostic is composed of thanksgiving elements from various other psalms. This psalm has been included in the liturgy of the three daily services of the Jewish tradition. Indeed, according to Talmudic teaching, whoever recites this psalm three times a day is assured a place in the world to come. Even if it cannot guarantee us that greatest of rewards, it can certainly help us express the thanks that is ours to sing, and enrich our journey through the life of this world.

We close this chapter with one last psalm. Though brief and uncomplicated, it is the most powerful expression of thanksgiving in the Book of Psalms. Reading it, we can feel the gratitude of its author and the sparks of thankfulness within us stirred into flame. Its musicality is clear, built into the images of the psalm. We feel it in its cadences and in its building intensity. No words of scripture express the thanks that can be ours better than the last of the psalms, the one we can characterize as the great symphony of thanksgiving:

¹Hallelujah.
Praise God in His sanctuary;
Praise Him in the firmament of His power.
²Praise Him for His mighty acts;
Praise Him according to His abundant greatness.
³Praise Him with the blast of the horn;
Praise Him with the psaltery and harp.
⁴Praise Him with the timbrel and dance;
Praise Him with stringed instruments and the pipe.

⁵Praise Him with the loud-sounding cymbals;
Praise Him with the clanging cymbals.
⁶Let every thing that hath breath praise the Lord.
Hallelujah.

# A PERSONAL AFTERWORD

"Of making many books there is no end." (*Koheleth/ Ecclesiastes* 12:12) According to Jewish tradition, King Solomon wrote these words in Jerusalem, very close to where I am sitting as I write this personal reflection.[1] Why does anyone write a book? One reason is to learn more about something that piques your curiosity. You want to find out more about something you know only a little. Then, suddenly, what you are studying seizes you powerfully and comes alive for you in a way you had not anticipated. Like a spelunker who gets lowered into a cave and discovers an entire world down below, you come up and want to tell everyone about it. The book writes itself through you.

At one point in my life I was given a remarkable gift: a period of time in which I could do virtually anything I wanted. I quickly recognized that I could use the time to do some sustained studying. As I reflected on what I wanted to learn about, I realized that I needed to know more about the Book of Psalms.

By the time I came to the end of my exploration of Psalms, I was compelled by them. Normally when you are beginning to write a book, you should decide on a plan for its content, perhaps sketch out an outline. In this case, I could not let go long enough to go through those planning formalities. I sat down to write a chapter and could not stop until I had put on paper everything I wanted to say. Or, perhaps, the psalms would not *let* me stop until they had exhausted everything I could do to give them expression. This book coursed through me in a way I have not experienced before. I suspect it is because I "discovered" something interesting in the psalms; but more importantly the psalms touched me deeply in a personal way, as I hope they now touch you.

When I began to explore the psalms, the first thing I discovered was that I had a deeper familiarity with them than I gave myself credit for at the time. I had sustained a relationship with Psalms my entire life. At the time I began this study I knew, of course, that portions of the prayer book that had been dear to me as far back as I can remember were taken directly from the psalms, though I did not recognize just how extensive that appropriation was.

There were other important associations. I remember being deeply moved by the psalms (Psalms 113–118) that were included in the holiday services in the *Hallel* (the set of psalms recited during the liturgy in praise of God) when I attended festival services as a child. "I shall not die, but live, / And declare the works of the Lord." (Psalm 118:17) "This is the day which the Lord has made; / we will rejoice and be glad in it." (Psalm 118:24) They moved me even though I could not have told you exactly what they meant or why they affected me as much as they did.

Those words continued to move me—and to reveal new levels of meaning to me—as I read them during the subsequent years. I encountered Psalms, as well, in the funeral services—most notably, indeed almost universally, the twenty-third Psalm and others as well. Happily it became my custom to recite a few of the psalms when it was my good fortune to return to Jerusalem. "I rejoiced when they said to me 'Let us go up to the house of the Lord'" (Psalm 122:1) and "Pray for the peace of Jerusalem. May all those who love her prosper." (Psalm 122:6) As I started this exploration, one of the first things I discovered was the way the psalms were already woven into the fabric of my life. I was just not aware of it consciously, nor could I have put the meaning of that association into words.

Maybe it was the memory of those powerful words from the *Hallel* that pulled me to the psalms. Whatever the impetus, I decided to dedicate my newly found time to really understanding what this otherwise unfamiliar book of the Bible was all about. As far as I was aware I was setting out on an intellectual exploration; unconsciously, perhaps, I was drawn into a deeper quest. During the time I had given myself to learn, my relationship to the psalms, and my need for them, changed dramatically.

What began as an exercise in learning became an experience of spiritual encounter. The dispassionate study of the psalms gave way to the impassioned use of *tillim* in the manner they were used by generations of Jews before me—imploring God to be of help. When I experienced a very painful stretch of my rabbinate, I turned to *tillim* to find strength. How to surmount obstacles and overcome hurdles? How to conduct myself in the presence of those whose wishes for me were not always for the best (or at least not the same wishes I had for myself). The psalms helped me begin to feel the "table had been prepared for me . . ." (Psalm 23:5), and that neither others' wishes and plans, nor even my own, were the last word in the direction of my journey.

Psalms became less and less a theoretical matter and more and more powerfully personal. I started out studying the psalms to learn what they meant to "them." I ended up reading *tillim* because of what they meant to me. And I found myself comforted by them and drawing strength from them.

By the end of the process I returned to a more "intellectual" mode as I tried to figure out what it was about the psalms that enabled them to comfort and strengthen generations of my people and to have the same effect on me. But that was later. In between I allowed myself to experience the psalms and their effect on me. I set aside study and I entered into a relationship with this remarkable text.

At the beginning of this time, my father became ill. I did not know enough yet to sit by his bedside and read psalms. But after a very brief illness, he suddenly and unexpectedly died. I found myself compelled to find a Book of Psalms and remain with his body, sitting and reading randomly from it. I was reading for him, of course, to protect his soul. "He will not suffer thy foot to be moved" (Psalm 121:3); "The sun shall not smite you by day nor the moon by night. . . ." (Psalm 121:6) And I was reading for myself to find strength to cope with my loss, and to face the challenge of that time and of the new stage in my life into which his death had thrust me. "Yea though I walk through the valley of the shadow of death I shall fear no evil. . . ." (Psalm 23:4) Psalms was talking personally for me now; and very powerfully to me.

At my father's funeral the words of the psalms that I had heard and read so often sounded different to me and had a striking effect on me. I found myself consoled from a very deep source and able to ascend out of "the valley of the shadow" in ways that perhaps I would not have without those precious words.

While we were still in mourning for my father, I learned to turn to Psalms for comfort and consolation. Then while we struggled with that loss, my wife's mother was stricken with a grave illness. As we cared for her over her long sickness, I recalled how my experience with my father's death had taught me how to see Psalms differently. I found myself sitting by her bedside with the book open. At her bedside, Psalms was clearly replaced by *Tillim*. Through the words of the book, I searched for ways to give voice to our hope for her recovery—and looked for strength to do for her what she needed from us. By this time I understood that my relationship with the Psalms had evolved beyond a simple and intellectual pursuit. I recognized that they had become my companion in the face of human need. We would need them soon enough to help us face our loss of her. Petition for strength in the face of illness became petition for strength in the face of death, and then, once again in such a short time, the search for comfort and consolation in the loss of a parent.

"Weeping may tarry for the night, / But joy cometh in the morning" (Psalm 30:6): a new community, a home—and the arrival of a beautiful baby girl. We held her for the first time and I found myself paraphrasing *Tillim* as I thanked God for making us the "joyful parents of this child." (Psalm 113:9)

Over the course of this journey I turned to Psalms over and over again to teach me, guide me, comfort me, and offer me strength, and then to help me celebrate. In retrospect I suspect that I intuited this quality in Psalms from the start of the project. Perhaps that is why I undertook it in the first place. I could never have predicted the many and different ways I would need the psalms in subsequent times. Nor could I have foreseen that what began—at least in my conscious awareness—as an intellectual exercise would evolve into a deep, spiritual engagement. Yet that is how it turned out. The journey was a far different one than I had anticipated; deeper, richer, and more rewarding.

The psalms accompanied me during a profoundly difficult time in my life—and then beyond it to fulfillment and joy. They helped me through multifaceted adversity and inexpressible happiness. They enriched an arid time with beauty. They nourished my soul and gave me strength. They helped me to express the greatest delight. Truly they became "a fortress of defense" (Psalm 31:3) for me in time of need, "a rock in whom I take refuge" (Psalm 18:3) in times of trouble and a "horn of exaltation" (Psalm 112:9) in times of rejoicing.

The Book of Psalms began as the object of curiosity, and became a beloved friend. It did for me what we all hope our friends will do for us. It offered advice, comfort, and hope. It consoled me in times of loss, and rejoiced with me in the days of fulfillment. Over this journey Psalms became a precious life companion. Through this book I hope it can become yours.

Jerusalem
22 Av 5759
August 4, 1999

# NOTES

## Chapter 2

1. Simon, Solomon, *More Wise Men of Helm* (New York: Behrman House, 1965), p. 76.
2. *Jerusalem Report,* Jan. 9, 1997, p. 11.
3. Agnon, S. Y., *Days of Awe* (New York: Schocken Books, 1948), p. 222.
4. *Jerusalem Report,* cited above.
5. Indeed, the practice of using amulets and talismans is still widespread among many groups of Jews to this day, including various Hasidic groups, Jews of North African descent, and many Jews from Sephardic communities.

## Chapter 6

1. The subject of enemies and the psalmist's rage against them highlights a difference in outlook between the Jewish and Christian traditions. Christian writers regularly make comment to the effect that Christians have difficulty with vengeance and violence in Psalms directed particularly against enemies (Roland & Murphy, *The Psalms Are Yours,* New York: Paulist Press, 1993, pp. 51–52). Entire psalms or sections of psalms are excluded from Christian liturgy or from the calendar of readings because of this discomfort. The *Apostolic Constitution* of the Catholic Church, issued in 1970, states:

In this new arrangement of the psalms some few of the psalms and verses which are somewhat harsh in tone have been omitted, especially because of the difficulties that are foreseen from their use in vernacular celebration.

The excluded sections or psalms consistently involve curses directed at enemies. C. S. Lewis characterizes these psalms as "terrible or (dare we say?) contemptible" (*Reflections on the Psalms*, New York: Harcourt Brace & Company, 1958, pp. 21–2), and ponders whether such sections should be read at all.

Christian difficulty with "material with negative import" (Holladay, p. 314) stems from a tradition of Jesus who taught "love your enemies and pray for those who persecute you" (Matthew 5:44) and "Love your enemies, do good to those who hate you, bless those who curse you, pray for those who abuse you. To him who strikes you on the cheek, offer the other cheek also; and from him who takes away your cloak, do not withhold your coat as well. . . ." (Luke 6: 27–29). A tradition steeped in such an ethic would have difficulty incorporating some of the sentiments articulated in the psalms.

There is no comparable Jewish anguish about reading psalms containing these sentiments, but it should be noted that there is plentiful material in the Hebrew scriptures that evinces attitudes diametrically at odds with those articulated in Psalms. One grouping has been suggested by C. S. Lewis (*Reflections on the Psalms*, p. 26):

> You shall not hate your kinsperson in your heart. You shall not bear a grudge against the children of your people . . . but you shall love your neighbor as yourself. (Leviticus 19:17–18)

> When you come upon your enemy's ox or ass wandering about, you must surely take it back to them. (Exodus 23:4)

> When you see the ass of one who hates you struggling under its burden—even if you would like to hold back from raising it up, nevertheless you must help raise it up. (Exodus 23:5)

Rejoice not when your enemies fall, and let your heart
not be glad when they stumble. (Proverbs 24:17)

If your enemy is hungry—give them bread and if they
are thirsty, give them water to drink. (Proverbs 25:21)

These last verses from Proverbs are traditionally attributed to King
Solomon in the same way that Psalms—especially the "enemy" references in Psalms—is ascribed to King David, his father. While many
attributes have been credited to David, zealous and passionate
among them, it is Solomon who is characterized as wise. From material like the verses above, a counter-tradition could be created.

Perhaps in response to some discomfort with the Psalms' reflex
to vengeance, *Midrash Tehillim* categorically states that "vengeance
will not be on common people, but only upon kings" (*Midrash
Tehillim* to Psalm 149), thus attempting to limit the scope of the calls
for retribution that occur in Psalms with such frequency.

Even with this, there has never been an impulse in Jewish tradition comparable to that in Christian tradition to edit or filter the
psalms, or to purge them of their evocation of the darker expressions of the human spirit.

## Chapter 7

1. We borrow the crucial verb here on the basis of analogy with a comparable verse in Isaiah (31:1).
2. Similar sentiments are expressed in Psalm 108:2–5.

## Afterword

1. He should know. Tradition ascribes three books of the Bible to him:
Song of Songs in his lusty youth, Proverbs in the prime of his wisdom, and *Koheleth*/Ecclesiastes as he bitterly encountered his latter
years.

# SUGGESTIONS FOR FURTHER READING

## Texts of the Psalms

*The Book of Psalms, A New Translation.* Philadelphia: Jewish Publication Society, 1972.

*Psalms I 1–50, Translation and Commentary* by Mitchell Dahood. New York: Doubleday and Co., 1966.

*The Psalms, Translation and Commentary* by Rev. Dr. A. Cohen. London: Soncino Press Ltd., 1945.

## Books about the Psalms

Holladay, William L. *The Psalms Through Three Thousand Years.* Minneapolis: Fortress Press, 1993.

Levine, Herbert J. *Sing unto God a New Song.* Bloomington: Indiana University Press, 1995.

Lewis, C. S. *Reflections on the Psalms.* New York: Harcourt Brace and Company, 1958.

Murphy, Ronald E. *The Psalms Are Yours.* New York: Paulist Press, 1993.

Sarna, Nahum M. *Songs of the Heart.* New York: Schocken Books, 1993.

Weintraub, Simkha Y. and the Jewish Healing Center. *Healing of Soul, Healing of Body: Spiritual Leaders Unfold the Strength & Solace in Psalms.* Woodstock, Vt.: Jewish Lights Publishing, 1994.

## A Brief Introduction to the Psalms

Hollander, John. "Psalms" in *Congregation,* ed. David Rosenberg, 293–312. San Diego: Harcourt Brace Jovanovich, 1987.

## Literary Treatments of the Psalms

Mitchell, Stephen. *A Book of Psalms.* New York: HarperCollins, 1993.

Rosenberg, David A. *A Poet's Bible.* New York: Hyperion, 1991.

# INDEX OF SCRIPTURAL REFERENCES

## Psalms

| | | | |
|---|---|---|---|
| 1:6 | *106* | 7:2–6 | *102* |
| 2 | *5* | 7:7 | *114* |
| 2:4 | *115* | 7:10 | *105* |
| 3 | *72, 126* | 7:16–17 | *122* |
| 3:7–9 | *126* | 9 | *148* |
| 3:8 | *114* | 9:20 | *114* |
| 4 | *34* | 10 | *34* |
| 6 | *34, 52, 88–91, 151* | 10:1 | *45* |
| | | 10:12 | *114* |
| 6:6 | *52* | 10:17 | *151* |
| 6:9–10 | *151* | 13 | *58–59, 100* |
| 6:11 | *88, 100* | 13:3–5 | *100, 110* |

| | | | |
|---|---|---|---|
| 13:5–6 | *34* | 23:5 | *102, 159* |
| 14 | *18* | 24 | *12* |
| 15 | *137* | 25 | *ix, 18, 155* |
| 16 | *17, 137* | 25:2 | *110* |
| 16:5–11 | *135* | 25:19–20 | *110* |
| 17 | *18* | 26 | *18* |
| 17:1 | *151* | 27 | *ix* |
| 17:8–9 | *100* | 27:1–6 | *128–129* |
| 17:12 | *103* | 28 | *18, 137* |
| 17:13 | *114* | 28:1–2 | *151* |
| 18 | *5, 18, 72, 126–128, 137, 162* | 28:4 | *123* |
| | | 28:5–6 | *34* |
| 18:1 | *13* | 28:6 | *154* |
| 18:3 | *162* | 29 | *144* |
| 18:4, 31–43, 49 | *126–128* | 30 | *35–36, 37–38, 84–85, 90, 137, 161* |
| 20 | *x, 72* | 30:2 | *100* |
| 20:2 | *73* | 30:6 | *37, 161* |
| 20:8 | *140* | 30:10 | *36, 52* |
| 22 | *18, 52–58* | 30:12 | *37, 38* |
| 23 | *x, 5, 102, 136–137* | 31 | *45* |
| | | 31:3 | *162* |
| 23:4 | *160* | 31:8–9 | *129* |

| | | | |
|---|---|---|---|
| 31:11–13 | *45* | 42:10–11 | *46* |
| 31:16 | *110* | 44 | *46* |
| 31:19–20 | *34* | 44:2–9 | *146–147* |
| 32 | *17, 18* | 44:7–8 | *180* |
| 32:6–7 | *34* | 44:12 | *114* |
| 33 | *72* | 44:24 | *46* |
| 34 | *141–144, 155* | 44:24–27 | *46* |
| 34:1–12, 16–23 | *34* | 44:27 | *46, 114* |
| 35 | *117–122* | 46 | *148* |
| 35:2 | *114* | 47 | *138, 148* |
| 35:15–16 | *119* | 48 | *12, 137, 140* |
| 35:23 | *114* | 49 | *72* |
| 37:13 | *115* | 50:19–20 | *103* |
| 38 | *18, 72, 85–90* | 52:3–6 | *102–103* |
| 38:13, 17, 20–21 | *100* | 52:3–11 | *105* |
| 40 | *145–146* | 52:4 | *113, 125* |
| 40:2–6 | *146* | 52:11 | *145* |
| 41 | *17, 72, 76–78, 137* | 52:22 | *125* |
| | | 54:4 | *125, 151* |
| 41:3, 6–12 | *100* | 54:6–7 | *129* |
| 41:4–5 | *72* | 54:8 | *145* |
| 42 | *17, 46* | 55:3 | *151* |
| | | 55:18 | *151* |

| | | | |
|---|---|---|---|
| 55:20 | *151* | 68:5–9 | *29–30* |
| 55:22 | *125* | 69:5 | *100, 121* |
| 56:12 | *140* | 69:17 | *145* |
| 57:3–4 | *109* | 71:24 | *104* |
| 57:5 | *103, 113, 125* | 74:1 | *45, 50* |
| 55:22 | *125* | 74:22 | *114* |
| 57:7 | *123* | 75:11 | *106* |
| 57:8–11 | *148–149* | 77 | *17* |
| 58:11–12 | *107* | 81 | *12* |
| 59 | *17, 111–117, 119, 121* | 82 | *12* |
| | | 82:8 | *114* |
| 59:8 | *125* | 84 | *72* |
| 61:1 | *151* | 86 | *18, 72* |
| 61:6 | *151* | 88 | *49–52* |
| 63:4 | *145* | 88:11–13 | *51* |
| 64 | *124–126* | 89 | *72, 101* |
| 64:2 | *151* | 89:39–46 | *101* |
| 64:4 | *113, 125* | 90 | *ix, 17, 72* |
| 65:3 | *151* | 90–108 | *72* |
| 66 | *148* | 91 | *138–139* |
| 67 | *72* | 91:11–12 | *73, 189* |
| 68 | *29* | 92 | *12, 149–150* |
| 68:2 | *114* | 93 | *12, 140* |

| | | | | |
|---|---|---|---|---|
| 94 | *12* | | 111:9 | *14* |
| 95–100 | *140* | | 112:9 | *102* |
| 102 | *47–48, 72* | | 113 | *25–26, 31, 161* |
| 103 | *ix, 18, 74–76, 141* | | 113–118 | *8, 31, 158* |
| | | | 113:5–9 | *26* |
| 103:3 | *72, 75* | | 113:7 | *14* |
| 103:13–16 | *72, 75* | | 113:9 | *161* |
| 104:33 | *148* | | 114 | *18, 27–29, 30, 31* |
| 105 | *17, 18* | | | |
| 106 | *82* | | 114:1–8 | *27* |
| 106:1 | *144* | | 114:5 | *60* |
| 107 | *72, 78, 81–85* | | 115 | *137* |
| 107:1 | *81, 144* | | 115:17 | *51* |
| 107:2–3 | *82* | | 116 | *150–151, 152–153* |
| 107:6, 13, 19, 28 | *73* | | 116:1 | *14* |
| | | | 117 | *137* |
| 108 | *18* | | 118 | *31–34, 72, 73, 82, 158* |
| 108:2–5 | *165* | | | |
| 109:3 | *121* | | 118:1 | *144* |
| 109:4–5 | *121–122* | | 118:8–9 | *140* |
| 109:21 | *145* | | 118:10–15 | *33* |
| 110 | *5* | | 118:17 | *158* |
| 111 | *18, 141, 155* | | 118:22 | *33* |

| 118:24 | 158 |
| 119 | 15, 72, 155 |
| 120 | 18 |
| 121 | x, 18, 137, 141, 160 |
| 121:2–4 | 114 |
| 121:3 | 160 |
| 121:6 | 160 |
| 121:8 | 14 |
| 122:1 | 159 |
| 123 | 18 |
| 124 | 18, 148 |
| 125:1–2 | 141 |
| 126 | 147 |
| 126:1 | 148 |
| 126:6 | 159 |
| 130 | x, 18 |
| 130:5 | 14 |
| 131:7 | 14 |
| 136 | 18, 82 |
| 136:1 | 144 |
| 137 | 5, 17 |
| 137:5–6 | 107 |
| 137:7–9 | 108 |
| 138 | 18 |
| 138:6–7 | 129, 152 |
| 139 | ix |
| 141 | 72 |
| 141:9–10 | 106 |
| 142 | 72 |
| 143 | 72 |
| 143:11–12 | 107 |
| 144 | 72 |
| 145 | 153–155 |
| 145:18 | 14 |
| 145:20 | 106 |
| 146:1–2 | 148 |
| 146:3 | 140 |
| 147:1 | 145 |
| 147:7 | 148 |
| 148 | 148 |
| 149 | 165 |
| 150 | 17, 155–156 |

Genesis

| 3:6 | 144 |
| 16:3 | 40 |

| 18:16–33 | 91 |
|----------|-----|
| 21:16 | 40 |
| 21:17–21 | 60 |
| 25:22 | 24 |
| 29:20 | 22 |
| 29–35 | 21 |
| 30:1 | 22 |
| 30:1–2 | 22 |
| 30:22–24 | 24 |
| 37:24–48 | 36 |
| 45:8 | 36 |

**Exodus**

| 1:20 | 62 |
|------|-----|
| 2:11–15 | 96 |
| 2:16–20 | 95 |
| 2:24 | 151 |
| 14:13 | 130 |
| 15:2–3 | 120 |
| 17:16 | 28 |
| 19:18 | 30 |
| 23:4 | 164 |
| 23:5 | 164 |
| 32:11–35 | 91 |

**Leviticus**

| 19:17–18 | 164 |
|----------|-----|

**Numbers**

| 12:13 | 66 |
|-------|-----|
| 20:11 | 28 |

**Deuteronomy**

| 25:5–7 | 62 |
|--------|-----|
| 32:39–43 | 120 |

**Ruth**

| 1:19–21 | 41 |
|---------|-----|
| 4:13–17 | 62 |

**2 Samuel**

| 22 | 5 |
|----|---|

**1 Kings**

| 19:1–4 | 97 |
|--------|-----|

**2 Kings**

| 4:18–19 | 66 |
|---------|-----|
| 20:1–6 | 69 |

## Ezra

3              *82*

## Esther

4:16           *134*

9:1            *123*

9:24–25        *123*

## Proverbs

24:17          *165*

25:21          *165*

## Ecclesiastes

12:12          *157*

## Isaiah

8:10           *130*

31:1           *165*

38:1–5         *70*